CHECK YOUR ENGLISH VOCABULARY FOR

LIVING
IN THE
UK

Rawdon Wyatt

A & C Black • London

www.acblack.com

First published in Great Britain 2006
Reprinted 2008

A & C Black Publishers Ltd
38 Soho Square, London W1D 3HB

A CIP entry for this book is available from the British Library
ISBN-10: 0 7136 7914 X
ISBN-13: 978 0 7136 7914 4

Text typeset by A & C Black
Printed in Great Britain at Caligraving Ltd, Thetford, Norfolk

This book is produced using paper that is made from wood grown in managed, sustainable forests. It is natural, renewable and recyclable. The logging and manufacturing processes conform to the environmental regulations of the country of origin.

Introduction

This book has been written for anyone coming to live and / or work in the United Kingdom, and who wants to:

- test and develop their knowledge of the key words and expressions that they might need or encounter on a day-to-day basis.
- learn about different aspects of the United Kingdom, including its history, politics, laws, rules, institutions and way of life.

The book contains exercises that present the vocabulary and information in a lively and interesting way. Crosswords, quizzes, gap-fills and other tasks mean that you will test and develop your knowledge in an active way.

When you use the book, you should not go through the exercises 'mechanically'. It is better to choose areas that are of particular interest, or areas that you feel would be particularly relevant to your needs.

The exercises are accompanied by a full key at the back. This not only gives you all the answers, but also provides you with a lot of other information that might be useful.

It is important to record new words and expressions that you learn. Try to develop your own personal vocabulary 'bank' in a notebook or file. Review the words and expressions on a regular basis so that they become a part of your 'productive' vocabulary.

You will find it very helpful to use a dictionary when you do the exercises. A good dictionary will give a clear definition of words and expressions, show you how they are pronounced, and give sample sentences that show how they are used in context. The Macmillan English Dictionary (ISBN 978-0333-964828) is particularly recommended, as it also provides a lot of background information on the United Kingdom and its various institutions.

Many of exercises and questions in this book are based on the things you will need to know if you are going to take the Home Office Life in the UK Test. The UK Home Office produces a very useful book called *Life in the United Kingdom: A Journey to Citizenship* (ISBN 978-0113-413027), which we recommend as a reference source. You might also like to consider the *British Citizenship Test Study Guide*, published by Red Squirrel Publishing (ISBN 978-0955-215919), which contains typical Citizenship Test questions.

One further resource, and one that would be particularly helpful when using this book, would be a detailed large-scale map of the United Kingdom. These are usually available from the travel section of any well-stocked bookshop.

While you are using this book, you should note that national rules and laws are constantly changing and evolving, and while the information in this book was correct when it went to print, there may have been changes since then. You can keep up to date by checking the website www.direct.gov.uk, which provides public service information from the UK government, and includes useful directories and links to on-line services.

This book is not an official text relating to the Home Office Life in the UK Test. For further information about all aspects of British Citizenship and the Life in the UK Test, visit www.lifeintheuktest.gov.uk.

Please also note that this book is not intended to provide advice of a statutory or regulatory nature, nor is it a statement of the law. For advice and assistance regarding employment, health and social welfare, legal and other matters, contact should be made with an appropriate body, such as Citizens' Advice.

Contents

Exercise 1: Complete these sentences with an appropriate abbreviation from the box. The meanings of these abbreviations are explained in the answer key.

AA ASBO BA BBC C of E GCSE GMT MP NHS
NSPCC PIN RAF RSPCA VAT

1. If you feel strongly about problems in the area you live in, you should write to your local _____.
2. The _____ produces and broadcasts a wide range of television and radio programmes.
3. During the war, he flew transport aircraft for the _____.
4. If you want to book a flight to Mumbai, you could try the _____ website to see if there are any good deals or special offers available.
5. When you use a credit or debit card in a shop, you will need to know your _____.
6. When they are 15 or 16 years old, children in England and Wales sit their _____ exams.
7. If you think your neighbour is treating his dog badly, you should call the _____.
8. And if you think he is being cruel to his children, you should call the police or the _____.
9. Our neighbour caused us so much trouble that eventually we asked the police to apply for a / an _____.
10. It's eight o'clock in the evening in Singapore, which means that it's midday _____.
11. The _____ is always short of doctors, nurses, beds, equipment and just about everything else they need.
12. Religious leaders say that there has been a sharp drop in attendance at _____ services.
13. The printer costs £100, plus _____ at 17.5%.
14. If you own a car, membership of an organisation such as the _____ is recommended.

Exercise 2: Instructions as above.

A and E BA BT CAB DVLA ESOL FCO
FE GP ID MOT NI PG TUC

1. You've had that cough for a long time. You should really go and see your _____.
2. The majority of telephone lines in the UK are provided by _____.
3. If you have a legal problem, it sometimes helps to talk to the _____, who might be able to give you some useful advice.
4. Before you start work, your employer will usually ask you for your _____ number.
5. A lot of workers' organisations in Britain are represented by the _____.
6. Some form of _____, such as a passport or driving licence, is often required in places such as banks, airports, etc.
7. All vehicles over three years old must have a valid _____ certificate to remain on the road.
8. If you come from outside the European Union and want to drive a car in Britain, you will need a driving licence that is recognised by the _____.

9. This film has a _____ rating, so some people may not want their children to watch it.
10. A lot of people who work also do an evening course at a / an _____ college.
11. British _____ certificates that are recognised around the world include PET, FCE, CPE and IELTS.
12. If you travel abroad, you can find lots of useful information on the _____ website.
13. If you have an accident or suddenly become ill and you require urgent medical treatment, you should try to get to the _____ department at your nearest hospital.
14. She left university after three years with a _____ in Modern Languages.

Exercise 3: Abbreviations are often used in small advertisements (called *classifieds* or *small ads*) in newspapers, especially when someone is renting / letting property, or selling a car. Look at the advertisements in the boxes, then complete the longer descriptions with words or expressions formed from the abbreviations in **bold**.

ATTRACTIVE furnished and **s/c one-bdrm** flat **nr** Woodstock. **CH**. All **mod cons**. **N/s** preferred. No pets. £700 **pcm inc** bills. **Dep** required. **Min** 6 **mth** let.

We have an attractive furnished and __________ one-__________ flat to rent __________ the town of Woodstock. The flat benefits from __________ and has all the __________ that you would expect in a property of this class. We would prefer you to be a __________. We will not allow pets in our property. The rent is £700 __________, which __________ bills. You will also need to pay a __________ when you move in. You will need to rent the flat for a __________ of six __________.

MAZDA MX5 1.8. Metallic black. 2002. **Exc** condition. **A/C**, **P/S**. Recently serviced. **FSH**. MOT until **e/o** year. £9500 **ono**.

I am selling my metallic black 2002 model Mazda MX5 1.8. It is in __________ condition. It has __________ to keep you cool in summer, and __________ which makes it easy to turn the car around. It has been serviced recently, and it has a __________ so that you know it has been well-maintained. The MOT is valid until the __________ the year. I am selling it for £9500, __________.

Cultural do's and don'ts

This exercise looks at some of the things that you should or should not do in the UK. In many cases, these will be the same in your country, but you might find some differences. Match the first part of each sentence on the left with its most appropriate second part on the right, then decide if each situation is **acceptable** or **unacceptable**. In some cases, this will depend on the nature of the situation. The first one has been done for you.

1. Arrive at someone's house empty-handed...
2. Ask someone about...
3. Ask someone how much...
4. Ask someone how old...
5. Belch after a meal...
6. Blow your nose...
7. Compliment someone...
8. Drive a car without showing courtesy...
9. Drop litter or spit...
10. Eat or drink while...
11. Eat with your...
12. Forget to say...
13. Greet someone without...
14. Hold hands or show gentle affection with...
15. Interrupt someone when they...
16. Leave a party or other social occasion without...
17. Make jokes...
18. Offer to split the bill at the end of...
19. Only buy drinks for yourself...
20. Open a present...
21. Point or stare...
22. Contradict or disagree...
23. Push into the queue...
24. Refusing to eat food...
25. Say "Eh?" or "What?" to someone if...
26. Smoke in someone's house...
27. Try to bring the price down...
28. Use humour and gentle irony when...
29. Use the toilet...
30. Walk into someone's house...
31. Whistle, click your fingers or shout...
32. Arrive slightly late when you are...

...they are.
...they earn.
...in front of other people.
...at a bus stop, in a shop, etc.
...walking along the street.
...for an informal party.
...when they have invited you for drinks, dinner, etc.
...without asking them for their permission first.
...their politics.
...are talking to you.
...you do not hear or understand them.
...in front of the person who has bought it for you.
..."Please" or "Thank you".
...on the ground.
...about someone's skin colour, religion, culture, sexuality, etc.
... shaking hands or kissing them.
...a meal in a restaurant.
...fingers.
...speaking with people you don't know very well.
...invited to an informal party.
...on their clothes or possessions.
...with your shoes on.
...with someone during a discussion.
...to get someone's attention in a pub, restaurant, shop, etc.
...at people.
...to other road users.
...when you are in the pub with friends.
...when you are buying something in a shop.
...to show your appreciation for the food.
...your boyfriend, girlfriend, husband, wife, etc, in public places.
...in a pub or restaurant if you are 'caught short' in the street.
...thanking your host for his / her hospitality.
...that is given to you, at a dinner party for example.

Education

Exercise 1: Complete sentences 1 – 18 with a word or words, and write these into the grid below. Some of the letters are already in the grid. If you do this correctly, you will reveal a two-word expression in the shaded vertical strip that can be used to complete sentence 19. Note that where an answer requires two words, you do not need to leave a space in the grid.

1.									U		S				
2.						S				E					
3.	C			D						O			L		
4.							R					Y			
5.						E			N						
6.							U				O				
7.				L	U					Y					
8.							B								
9.					M				H						
10.		E		I					S						
11.									E	E					
12.							U				E				
13.									G	H					
14.							G								
15.						N	G					S			
16.							A						S		
17.		P	R						T						
18.						C				U			O		

1. Many children begin their educational development at a __________ school (also called a *kindergarten*) from the age of 3.
2. Most schools in the UK are __________ schools: they are supported with money from the government and provide free education for children.
3. Most schools in the UK are _____-_____, which means that girls and boys are educated together.
4. Between the ages of 5 and 11, children go to __________ school.
5. Between the ages of 11 and 16, 17 or 18, children go to __________ school.
6. Although education is free, parents are expected to pay for their child's school __________ and sports wear.
7. Schools often ask parents to make __________ contributions for school activities, but children will not be excluded from these activities if the parents cannot or will not make these payments.
8. Independent schools are privately run, but are often confusingly called __________ schools.
9. All schools ask parents to sign a 'contract' known as a _____-_____ agreement, in which both parents and the school promise to do everything they can to help children with their education.
10. All schools have to run __________ education classes, but parents can withdraw their children from these classes if they want.
11. All children receive __________ advice from their schools from the age of 14.
12. When they are 16 or 17, many young people go to their local college to continue with their education or learn a skill. This is known as __________ education, and is free for people up to the age of 19.

13. The answer to number 12 above should not be confused with __________ education, which is education at a university or at a college of a similar level.
14. At the age of 16, most children in England and Wales take their __________ examinations before either leaving school or continuing with their education.
15. People who want to develop and improve their English can join an ESOL course at a local college. ESOL is an abbreviation for *English for Speakers of Other* __________.
16. Students who continue with their secondary education until they are 18 take exams called _____-_____: they will normally need these to get into university.
17. If parents fail to ensure their children go to school, they could be __________. In extreme cases, this might involve a prison sentence.
18. Education is free and __________ for all children between the ages of 5 and 16.
19. State schools have to follow the __________ __________, which covers such subjects as English, mathematics, science, history, geography, foreign languages, etc.

Exercise 2: Choose the correct word or words in **bold** to complete these sentences.

1. After leaving school, and before going to university, many young people take a / an **gap** / **space** / **open** year (= a year out of education) in order to get work experience, earn money or travel.
2. Students apply for a place at university in January or February, and **encroachment** / **entrapment** / **enrolment** usually takes place in September.
3. A student at university for the first time is called a / an **graduate** / **undergraduate** / **pre-graduate**.
4. Students in England and Wales are expected to pay money towards their tuition **fees** / **fares** / **prices** (in Scotland they are free).
5. Students who need help paying for their university course can apply for a government **lend** / **loan** / **lease**.
6. Some students in exceptional circumstances might receive a **grant** / **grunt** / **gaunt** to help pay for their course.
7. A BA is one of the types of degree that students work towards at university. BA stands for **Britannicus Achievius** / **Briton of Authority** / **Bachelor of Arts**.
8. A talk given to a class of students at university is known as a **lesson** / **lecture** / **lectern**.
9. A meeting of a small group of university students to discuss a subject with a teacher is called a **semester** / **semolina** / **seminar**.
10. A teaching session between a teacher and one or more students at university is called a **tutorial** / **tutelage** / **tutor**.
11. A / an **ante-graduate** / **postgraduate** / **graduate-plus** is someone who is studying after receiving a first university degree.
12. Because so many students find exams stressful, many universities combine exam results with a process of **continuing** / **continual** / **continuous** assessment in order to grade their students at the end of a course of study.

Employment 1: Job applications

Look at the pairs of words and expressions in **bold** in this article, and decide which one is best in each situation. In several cases, *both* words are correct.

Part 1

When a company has a (1) **vacancy / vacant** for a job, and it needs to (2) **hire / recruit** a new member of (3) **crew / staff**, it usually (4) **publicises / advertises** the (5) **post / position**. It does this (6) **internally / internationally** (for example, in the company magazine or on a company notice board, so that the job is only open to people already working for the company), or (7) **extensively / externally** in the 'situations vacant' section of a newspaper. It might also use a recruitment (8) **agency / agenda**, which helps people to find (9) **job / work**, or in a Jobcentre (which can be found in most large towns). Companies that have their own website will also list available jobs on that website.

A job advertisement has to give an accurate (10) **describing / description** of the job and what the company needs and expects from the (11) **applicant / application** (the person who is (12) **applying / appalling** for the job). These (13) **requirements / requisitions** might include (14) **qualifications / qualifiers** (academic, vocational or professional), (15) **experience / experiences** in similar lines of work, and personal (16) **qualifications / qualities** (for example, it might say that you need to be (17) **practicing / practical**, (18) **professional / professorial** and have a sense of humour).

Most advertisements specify the (19) **rewards / remuneration** that the company can offer in return for your work (including the basic annual (20) **wage / salary**, any commission you could receive, regular pay (21) **rises / increments**, and so on). Some advertisements will also tell you about other (22) **benefits / beneficiaries** (including paid annual (23) **leave / holidays**, free medical care, a company car, free meals in the cafeteria, etc) that you might receive. If the (24) **packet / package** they are offering is very generous and attractive, and is (25) **commensurate/ commendable** with the work that is necessary, the company can expect a lot of people to apply for the job.

Note that a company cannot (26) **disseminate / discriminate** against someone because of their sex, nationality, race, colour, ethnic group, religion, sexuality or age, or because they have a (27) **disablement / disability**. Any company that rejects someone on these grounds (either in their job advertisement, during the application process, when they meet the person concerned, or when that person is already working for them) is breaking the law.

Part 2

If somebody is interested in the job, they are usually asked to send to send their (1) **curriculum vitae / résumé** (which should give details of their education, the points mentioned in numbers 14 and 15 above, and any skills or interests that might be relevant for the job they are applying for). This should be accompanied by a (2) **cover / covering** letter (also called a *letter of introduction*). This should be typed rather than handwritten, and it should explain briefly why they are applying for the job and why they think they would be (3) **suiting / suitable** for it. Alternatively, they might be asked to (4) **fill in / fill**

out an (5) **application / applicant** form and (6) **submit / send** it to the company. The managers of the company will read these and then make a (7) **short-list / small-list** of the people they would like to attend an (8) **interrogation / interview**. At the same time, they will (9) **reject / turn down** those who they feel are (10) **unsuitable / unthinkable**.

The people who are responsible for choosing a new employee will consider the different aspects of the (11) **candidates / applicants** to decide whether they have the correct (12) **potency / potential** for the job. In addition to the points mentioned in 14 and 15 above, these might include physical (13) **apparition / appearance** (are they smart and well-presented?), general (14) **disposition / disposal** (for example, are they friendly and easy to work with?), special (15) **skills / abilities** (for example, are they computer (16) **literate / numerate**, can they drive, or do they speak any other languages?) and (17) **interests / hobbies** (what do they like doing in their free time?). They might also consider their family (18) **backing / background** and (19) **medicine / medical** history, although it is illegal to refuse someone a job on these grounds. At the same time, they will probably check on their work history and qualifications (which is why it is very important to be honest when being interviewed), and may also check to see if they have a (20) **criminal / crime** record. In addition, they may also ask to see some form of (21) **identity / identification**, and a work (22) **permit / permission** if the person applying for the job does not have British citizenship or comes from a country outside the European Union. The person who most closely (23) **suits / matches** the (24) **profile / criteria** decided by the managers will then be accepted for the job.

Before somebody is (25) **offered / suggested** the job, s/he is asked to provide (26) **referees / references** from people who know him / her (usually a former (27) **employer / employee**, a (28) **colleague / co-worker**, and / or a teacher or college tutor). Before s/he actually starts working, s/he may go through an (29) **induction / introduction** programme to learn more about the company and the job. Sometimes, s/he may be given a (30) **temporary / temporal** contract and obliged to complete a (31) **trial / probationary** period (where his / her employers make sure that s/he is suitable for the job) before being offered something that is more (32) **permanence / permanent** (a *fixed-term* or *open-ended* contract, for example). On-the-job (33) **training / trainers** may also be offered or required. After s/he has been with the company for a while, there will probably be an (34) **appraisal / appreciable**, to assess how s/he is getting on. These may be repeated on a regular basis throughout his / her time with the company.

Employment 2: Earnings, rewards and benefits

Complete the first part of each word in **bold** in sentences 1 – 35 with the second part from the box.

-an	-ance	-ance	-ance	-ans	-ary	-ated	-ation	-ax	-ay	-ber
-ble	-count	-ction	-dancy	-den	-dex	-diture	-ement	-ensurate	-enue	-eration
-ernity	-ernity	-et	-faction	-fit	-ge	-hting	-imum	-ional	-ission	-kage
-ked	-lement	-me	-nefit	-nus	-ome	-ormance	-oss	-ployment	-ring	-roll
-se	-shake	-sion	-slip	-te	-time	-tive	-toms	-turn	-ve	

1. A wage is money that is normally paid to an employee on a weekly basis, and a **sal____** is money that is usually paid to an employee monthly on a regular basis.
2. **Remun____** is the formal word for money that an employee receives for doing his / her job.
3. When we work for more than the normal working time, we say that we work (and therefore earn) **over____**. An employer cannot make a worker do this if he /she does not want to.
4. An automatic and regular increase in pay is called an **incr____**.
5. **T____** is automatically removed from the money you receive and paid directly to the government department responsible for collecting it (HM **Rev____** and **Cus____**)
6. The government department in number 5 above may sometimes ask you to fill in a tax **re____**, which gives details of your financial situation.
7. **Nat____ Insur____** (NI) is a system that all employers and workers in the UK pay into. The money for this is automatically taken from the money you earn, and provides funds for things such as health services. Every worker in the country should have an NI **num____**.
8. Money that is removed from our earnings to pay for numbers 5 and 7 above, is called a **dedu____**.
9. The **min____ wa____** is the lowest hourly wage which an employer can legally pay its employees. An employer which pays less than this amount is breaking the law.
10. Time for which work is paid at twice the normal rate (for example, on national holidays) is called **dou____ ti____**.
11. A **pen____ pl____** helps people to save money for when they retire from work.
12. When you want more money for the work you do, you might ask your boss for a **ri____**.
13. If an employee needs some of his / her wages paid before the usual pay day, he / she might ask for an **adv____** (also called a *sub*).
14. A **pay____** shows an employee how much pay he / she has received, and how much has been removed for tax, insurance, etc.
15. An extra payment made in addition to a normal payment (usually received by sales people for selling more than their quota) is called a **bo____**.
16. A **pay____** is the list a company keeps that shows all the people employed and paid by that company.
17. A rewards **pac____** is the money and other benefits offered with a job.

18. A **weig**____ is an additional amount of money paid to an employee to compensate him / her for living in an expensive area.
19. By law, British companies have to give their employees the right to take paid holidays and other time off work: this is known as **lea**____ **entit**____.
20. **Inc**____ is another word for the money that people receive for working. The money that they spend is known as **expen**_____.
21. For some people, the money that they earn for doing a job is less important than job **satis**____ (the pleasure they get from doing their job).
22. A sales person usually earns a percentage of the sales value of the product or service he / she sells: this is called a **comm**_____.
23. Some companies have **incen**____ **pl**____, where they offer their employees extra rewards and benefits for good attendance, increased productivity, etc.
24. The amount of money an employee receives each hour, day, week, etc, is known as an hourly / daily / weekly **ra**____.
25. If an employee loses his / her job because the company doesn't need or can't afford to keep him / her, they should normally receive **redun**____ **p**____.
26. Some companies offer their employees a **dis**____ on the products and services they sell, which means that the employee can buy them for less than the usual price.
27. If an employee takes a job in another town or city which is a long way from his / her original home and place of work, he / she might be offered a **reloc**____ **allow**____.
28. Some companies have a policy of **pro**____ **sha**____, where some or all of the money that they make is given to their employees.
29. **Gr**____ is an adjective used to describe an employee's earnings before the money in numbers 5 and 7 on the previous page have been removed.
30. **N**____ is an adjective used to describe an employee's earnings after the money in numbers 5 and 7 on the previous page have been removed.
31. When the money that an employee receives rises automatically by the percentage increase in the cost of living, we say that it is **in**____**-lin**____.
32. If the amount of money an employee receives depends on how well he / she does his / her job, we say that it is **perf**____ – **rel**____.
33. When the money that an employee earns is based on age, experience, qualifications, position in the company, etc, we say that it is **comm**____.
34. Women who are expecting a baby are entitled to **mat**_____ leave before and after their child is born. Their partner is entitled to **pat**_____ leave.
35. People who do not have a job may be entitled to **unem**_____ **be**____, on certain conditions (for example, they have made enough NI contributions: see number 7 on the previous page).

Employment 3: Workplace issues

Complete sentences 1 – 15 with an appropriate word or words, and write these in the grid at the bottom of the page. If you do this correctly, you will reveal a two-word expression in the shaded vertical column that can be used to complete sentence 16. The first letter of each word is already in the grid.

1. A _____ _____ is an organisation of workers that aims to improve pay and conditions of work.
2. The _____ age for men is 65, and for women it is 60, although this will gradually rise to 65 by 2020.
3. Employers and workers must obey _____ _____ _____ regulations that exist to protect them.
4. If you fail to do your job properly, you will (in the first instance) be given a _____ _____ by your company.
5. _____ of any kind, including sexual and racial, is against the law.
6. If you are unhappy at work for any reason, the first person you should speak to is your _____.
7. If you lose your job because your company no longer needs you, or can no longer afford to employ you, you might receive _____ _____ to compensate you for loss of earnings.
8. If you are given _____ *to leave*, you are dismissed from your job.
9. Persistent lateness and _____ are unacceptable, and you might lose your job as a result.
10. Someone who works for him or herself can be described as _____-_____.
11. Women who are expecting a baby are entitled to _____ _____ of at least 18 weeks.
12. Sexual _____ in the workplace is against the law, whether it is done by a man or by a woman.
13. _____ is a general word which refers to any act carried out by a worker which is against company rules and regulations.
14. Strict laws exist to prevent the _____ of children in the workplace and elsewhere.
15. People who have lost their job and are looking for work can claim a benefit called a Jobseeker's _____.
16. If you have been told to leave your job through no fault of your own, and believe that you have a case for _____ _____, you can take your case to an employment tribunal.

1.							T					U								
2.				R																
3.	H						A			S										
4.					V						W									
5.							D													
6.								S												
7.							R									P				
8.									N											
9.										A										
10.							S				E									
11.						M									L					
12.							H													
13.										M										
14.					E															
15.										A										

Test your knowledge with this general knowledge quiz.

1. True or false: The UK is a union of four countries: England, Scotland, Wales and Ireland.
2. Rearrange the letters in **bold** to make words:
   The full name of the UK is the **nitdUe nodimgK of retGa tariBin and erotNnhr redlIna**.
3. True or false: *Great Britain* is another name for the UK.
4. Is there just one government for the whole of the UK?
5. Who is the *Head of State* of the UK?
6. Where might you expect to hear *Welsh* being spoken? Where might you expect to hear *Gaelic* being spoken?
7. Would you be making a mistake if you called someone from Scotland, Wales or Northern Ireland '*English*'?
8. What are the principal (capital) cities of Scotland, Wales and Northern Ireland?
9. What is the population of the UK (based on the 2001 census)?
   (a) About 25 million (b) About 36 million (c) About 49 million (d) About 59 million (e) About 72 million
10. True or false: There are more people in the UK aged 60 or over than there are aged 16 or under.
11. Match the ethnic groups on the left with their relevant population percentage figures on the right:

White	0.4%
Mixed	2%
Asian or Asian British	92%
Black or Black British	0.4%
Chinese	4%
Other	1.2%

12. What is the largest ethnic minority in the UK?
13. Where would you find the single biggest concentration (45%) of ethnic minorities in the UK?
14. What percentage of people in the UK say that they have a religion?
    (a) 98% (b) 86% (c) 75% (d) 62% (e) 50% (f) 42% (g) 30%
15. Rearrange the letters in **bold** to make the names of the most common religious faiths in the UK:
    hudBimsd hmikSis imnuHids smIal nthritiCiyas imaudJs
16. What percentage of people in the UK who have a religion say that they are *Christians*?
17. What percentage of the people in number 16 above say that they go to church regularly?
18. In which year did the Church of England come into existence?
    (a) 1066 (b) 1215 (c) 1485 (d) 1534 (e) 1642 (f) 1707
19. What and who is the *Supreme Governor*?
20. Identify the word in the following group that does not belong with the others, and explain why:
    Anglican Baptist Quaker Methodist Catholic Presbyterian
21. How far is it (in miles) from the north coast of Scotland to the south coast of England?
22. How far is it (in miles) across the widest part of the United Kingdom, from the west coast of Wales to the east coast of England?
23. In which UK cities might you expect to hear the following dialects and accents?:
    (a) Geordie (b) Brummie (c) Scouse (d) Cockney (e) Glaswegian

24. Below is a list of the fifteen largest cities in the UK (in terms of population). The first part of each city is in the left-hand box, and the second part is in the right-hand box. Match the two parts of each city together.

Lon...	Birmi...	Le...
Glas...	Shef...	Brad...
Edin...	Liver...	Manch...
Bris...	Card...	Cove...
Leice...	Bel...	Notti...

...ntry	...ester	...iff
...field	...fast	...burgh
...ngham	...ster	...ford
...gow	...pool	
...ngham	...tol	...don
...eds		

25. What is the minimum age for voting in a UK election?

26. Which of the following are not recognised UK political parties?

> The Red Lion   The Scottish National Party (the SNP)   Sinn Fein
> The Conservative Party   The Green Party   The Rose and Crown
> The British National Party (the BNP)   The Liberal-Democrats   Plaid Cymru
> The Ulster Unionist Party   The Social Democratic and Labour Party (the SDLP)
> The White Hart   The Labour Party

27. What sector of industry accounts for the largest proportion of GDP (gross domestic product) in the UK?

28. Approximately what percentage of the UK's able-bodied population of working age is unemployed?
(a) 5% (b) 8% (c) 12% (d) 15% (e) 20% (f) 24%

29. Do young people in the UK have to do compulsory military service?

30. Can women join the armed forces?

31. Approximately what percentage of women with children of school age are in paid work?
(a) 25% (b) 35% (c) 45% (d) 55% (e) 65% (f) 75% (g) 85%

32. Can a company or business legally pay women less than it pays men for doing the same job, or can it legally refuse to employ them because of their sex?

33. Are drugs such as cocaine, heroin, marijuana and ecstasy legal in the UK?

34. Does the UK have *capital* and / or *corporal* punishment?

35. What proportion of young people go on to higher education after they have finished school?
(a) 1 in 3 (b) 1 in 5 (c) 1 in 10 (d) 1 in 15 (e) 1 in 20

36. How old do you need to be in the UK to:
(a) Buy and smoke cigarettes?
(b) Buy and drink alcohol?
(c) Drive a car?
(d) Get married with your parents' permission?
(e) Get married *without* your parents' permission ?
(f) Join the armed forces?
(g) Have sexual relations with a member of the same or opposite sex?

Exercise 1: UK food has a bad reputation abroad, even with people who have never eaten it (the President of a European country famously said that we have the world's second worst food after Finland!). However, this reputation is not really justified, as there are many delicious national and regional dishes that are worth trying.

Match the names of some popular dishes 1 – 26 in the first box with their description A – Z in the second box.

(1) bangers and mash (2) black pudding (3) bubble and squeak (4) butty or sarnie (5) Cheddar, Cheshire, Wensleydale, Lancashire and Red Leicester (6) Christmas dinner (7) Cornish pasty (8) cream tea (9) fish and chips (10) full English (11) haggis (12) hot cross bun (13) Irish stew (14) Lancashire hotpot (15) mince pies (16) ploughman's lunch (17) sausage roll (18) shepherd's pie (19) steak and kidney pie (20) Sunday roast (21) tatties and neeps (22) tikka masala (23) toad-in-the-hole (24) trifle (25) Welsh rabbit (26) Yorkshire pudding

A. Sausages baked in a mixture of eggs, flour and milk.

B. A breakfast of cereal and fruit juice, followed by bacon, eggs, sausages and mushrooms, and finished with toast and jam or marmalade. Accompanied with tea or coffee.

C. A traditional family lunchtime meal of meat and potatoes cooked in an oven, and served with vegetables and gravy.

D. Sausages and mashed potato, traditionally served with onion gravy.

E. A traditional Scottish food, made from the inner organs of a sheep that are cut into small pieces, mixed with grain and pushed into the skin of a sheep's stomach before being cooked.

F. A Scottish mixture of potatoes and turnips, often eaten with *haggis*.

G. Pastry filled with fruit and spices and then baked, usually eaten at Christmas.

H. A small meal eaten in the afternoon, consisting of tea with *scones* (a sweetened bread-like food), jam and thick cream.

I. A thick soup made from lamb, potatoes, onions and other root vegetables.

J. A thick soup made from meat (usually lamb) and vegetables, topped with sliced potato and cooked in an oven until the potatoes go crispy.

K. A thick sausage made from pig's meat and blood, traditionally sliced and fried, and eaten for breakfast.

L. A sweet food made from cake, covered with fruit, jelly, custard and sometimes cream.

M. A traditional family lunchtime meal of roast meat (usually turkey), roast potatoes and parsnips, served with vegetables and gravy, and followed by a steamed fruit-based pudding.

N. Flour, milk and eggs mixed together, baked in an oven and usually served with roast beef.

O. The most famous British takeaway food! Battered, deep-fried seafood (usually cod) served with deep-fried potato strips. Typically eaten straight out of the bag it is wrapped in.

P. Cooked potatoes and other vegetables (especially cabbage), which are mixed together and then fried. A popular way of using up leftover vegetables.

Q. Informal words for a *sandwich*.

R. Minced lamb in a thick gravy, covered with mashed potato and baked in an oven.

S. A simple meal of bread, cheese (or sometimes cold meat), pickles and salad (often served with an apple).

T. Meat (beef) in a thick gravy, topped with pastry and baked in an oven.

U. A small tube of pastry with pork sausage meat inside, baked in an oven.

V. A small pie for one person, with meat, potatoes and other vegetables inside.

W. Popular types of British cheese.
X. Toast, covered with a cheese-based sauce and cooked under a grill.
Y. A sweet cake for one person, containing dried fruit and spices, traditionally eaten at Easter.
Z. A meat dish combining British and Indian ingredients (cream, yoghurt, spices, etc), developed by Indian chefs for British tastes.

Exercise 2: People from the UK travel abroad a lot for their holidays, and as a result have developed a taste for foreign food. This, coupled with an influx of immigrants to the UK in the 50's and 60's, has resulted in a huge range of foreign foods becoming available and popular throughout the country.

Look at the different food groups and dishes / ingredients below (these are the most popular ones that you will find in the UK), and identify the one word or expression in each group that does not belong with the others (because it does not originate in that country or area).

1. Italian:
focaccia, tortellini, polenta, couscous, minestrone, spaghetti, cannelloni, carpaccio.

2. Indian & South Asian:
naan, chapati, dhal, jalfrezi, dopiaza, passanda, vindaloo, tagine, balti.

3. Chinese:
chow mein, spring roll, chop suey, goulash, prawn wanton, egg fried rice, spare ribs, dim sum.

4. Lebanese & Middle-Eastern:
kebab, falafel, jerk chicken, houmous, tabbouleh, kibbeh, baba ganouje, khubz bread.

5. Japanese:
saganaki, sashimi, teriyaki, yakitori, tempura, sukiyaki, miso, wasabi.

6. French:
chicken chasseur, cassoulet, boeuf bourgignon, salad niçoise, bratwurst, escargots, tapénade, soufflé.

7. Spanish:
tapas, tortilla de patata, paella, caviar, gazpacho, chorizo, jamon Serrano, emparedados.

8. Mexican:
mole, tamales, fajitas, quesadillas, burritos, tacos, kimchi, enchiladas.

9. Greek:
pitta, stifado, blini, kleftiko, tzatziki, baklava, taramasalata, horiatiki

10. South-East Asian:
chicken satay, piri-piri chicken, nasi goreng, beef rendang, mee goreng, laksa, gado-gado, otak otak.

Exercise 1: Complete sentences 1 – 18 with a word(s) or number from the box. There are some words / numbers that do not fit in any of the sentences.

• 100 • 112 • 999 • 118118 • ambulance • A and E • ASBO • conscription • cure • dispensary • fitness centre • GP • health authority • health check • health club • HP • MA • medical card • mental • NHS • NHS Direct • patient • paramedics • pharmacist • prescription • register • specialist • surgery • treatment

1. The __________, set up in 1948, is a system that provides free medical care and is paid for through taxes.

2. A family doctor is also known as a __________.

3. A family doctor will normally work in a health care centre, sometimes also known as a __________.

4. Family doctors are responsible for providing most of the __________ for any illnesses that you may have.

5. This includes __________ as well as physical illness.

6. If they are unable to __________ you, they will usually refer you to a __________.

7. Before you see a doctor for the first time, you will need to __________ with your local health care centre.

8. In order to do this, you will need a __________.

9. These are available from your local __________ (you can find the telephone number in the phone book, or from your local library).

10. Unlike many other countries, there are a lot of medicines that you cannot buy 'over the counter' in a shop: you might need to get a __________ from your doctor.

11. You either take this to the __________ in the health care centre, or to the nearest chemist, where a trained __________ will prepare the medicine for you.

12. In an emergency (for example, an injury), you should go to the __________ department in your nearest hospital.

13. If you are unable to get there yourself, and if no one else can take you, you should call for an __________.

14. The number you need to call for one of these is __________ (or alternatively you can call __________). Remember, however, that these numbers are for genuine emergencies only.

15. The people who drive these are called __________, and they can often provide a range of emergency treatments (or take you to the hospital if they are unable to treat you on the spot).

16. A person receiving medical treatment is called the __________.

17. When you register with a doctor for the first time, you are entitled to a free __________.

18. __________ is a free 24-hour health information service which can give advice on various health issues. If you need advice, or are feeling ill, you can call them on 0845 4647.

Exercise 2: Look at these conversations, and rearrange the letters in **bold** to make words.

1. Receptionist (*on telephone*): Hello, Wheatley Health Care Centre.
Mr Harrison: Good morning. I'd like to make an **pomitnptaen** to see a doctor, please.

2. Foreign patient: I afraid my English is no so good. What I can do?
Receptionist: We can provide an **enirtretrep** when you see the doctor, but it might take a few days to arrange.

3. Doctor: Hello, come in and take a seat. What can I do for you?
Patient: I haven't been feeling very well for a couple of weeks.
Doctor: OK, well describe your **mspsotym** and I'll see what I can do.

4. Patient: I've got a pain in my abdomen. I'm sure I've got a hernia.
Doctor: I'm the doctor, Mrs Thompson. Just relax and let me make the **ianisdogs**.

5. Mrs Hunt (*on telephone to health care centre*): My son isn't feeling very well. Can you send a doctor?
Receptionist: I'm afraid we can only do **oeuhs slalc** if the situation is very urgent. Is it, do you think?

6. Patient: I don't want anyone else to know I've been here today.
Doctor: Don't worry, Ms Hamilton. Your visit will be treated in complete **fincdecnoe**.

7. Patient: I'm going to Sri Lanka next month, and I was wondering if I need any **aintaocnvcis** before I go.
Doctor: Well, at the moment we recommend that you protect yourself against diphtheria, tetanus and hepatitis A, and you should also take something that will help protect you from malaria.

8. Patient: Will I need to pay for the medicine on this prescription?
Doctor: Yes, there's a small charge, but you won't need to pay it if you're under 16, if you're under 19 and in full-time education, if you're pregnant or if you're on **mnoiec pupsort**.

9. Patient: Am I very ill?
Doctor: I don't think so, Mr Withers, but I'm going to refer you to the hospital. Take this note to the **tou-atiptsen** department at the Warton Hospital and they can check you out more thoroughly.

10. Mr Searle (*on telephone to hospital*): When can I come and see my wife? Her name's Alice Searle. She's in maternity.
Nurse: **tigisinV ruhos** are from nine in the morning until six in the evening, but if you can't make those times, we can arrange something for you.

11. Ms Buss: I need to see a **itetdsn**. One of my fillings has fallen out.
Receptionist: I'm afraid we're fully booked for two days. Is Wednesday all right?

12. Mr Mangat: I'm having some problems seeing things that are very close to me.
Doctor: Hmm, it sounds like you ought to see an **cipotnia** and get an eye test.

13. Doctor: Congratulations Mrs Johnson. You're pregnant.
Mrs Johnson: I thought so. That's wonderful news. So what happens next?
Doctor: Well, I'll arrange for you to see one of our registered **vdmiseiw**, who can tell you all about it.

14. Mrs Woods: Do you think I should have my baby at home?
Doctor: Well, normally we recommend having it in hospital, especially if it's your first baby, in case there are **molincacoptis**.

Exercise 1: Complete sentences 1 – 14 with words and expressions from the box.

• bills • borrowing • cable • cash • Ceefax • The Citizens' Advice Bureau • clubs • computer • DAB • digital • directions • directory • DVDs • entertainment • events • freeview • Google • government • Internet • Internet café • libraries • licence • local newspapers • lost • maps • membership • national newspapers • National Savings and Investments • organisations • parcels • passport • police officer • police station • post office • property • reference • satellite • search engine • sporting • stations • subscription • tax • Teletext • terrestrial • Thomson Local • tourist information centre • vehicles • website • Yahoo • Yellow Pages

1. If you want to find a telephone number for a person or company in your area, you should look in a telephone __________.

2. The __________ is a book containing the names, telephone numbers and (usually) the addresses of businesses and __________ in your area.

3. The __________ is a book which gives information on a wide range of local services and businesses, and often includes __________ of local towns, details about local __________ and organisations, etc.

4. __________ will keep you informed about what is happening nationally and internationally, as well as reporting on major __________ events and entertainment.

5. __________ are a good place to look for information on things such as __________ to rent or buy and __________ for sale, as well as letting you know about local news and __________.

6. Most large towns and cities have a __________, which can tell visitors about local events and places of interest, as well as giving information about local public transport, etc.

7. __________ and __________ are information services which can be accessed on most televisions.

8. There are many local and national radio __________ providing music, __________ and news 24 hours a day. Many of these are __________ stations, which means that they can only be received by digital radios.

9. There are five __________ television channels (*BBC1*, *BBC2*, *ITV*, *Channel 4* and *Channel 5*) which can be received on ordinary televisions. However, this is now changing, and it will soon be necessary to have __________ television equipment to receive any television station. Many television services are __________, which means that you do not need to pay to watch them. You need to pay a __________ in order to watch other __________ and __________ broadcasts. If you have a television in your home, you must have a television __________.

10. Each major town or city has at least one __________, which can give you free information on a huge range of topics, including consumer rights, healthcare and money matters.

11. __________ are not just for __________ books. Many now have CDs and __________ which members can take out, as well as __________ facilities. Most will have a __________ section containing books and guides that you can read on the premises, but which you cannot remove from the building. They will also have most of the books and guides mentioned in numbers 1 – 5 above. __________ of libraries is free, as are most of the services they provide.

12. If you are __________ or need __________ in a town or city, you can ask a __________ to help you (or if you cannot see one, you can go to the nearest __________ for help).

13. Your local __________ is not just a place where you can send letters and __________. In addition to many other things, you can __________ cheques, pay __________, pay for your road __________, and get various forms that you might need (for example, a __________ application form). You can also save your money at the post office, using __________ (a __________ -backed service)

14. The _________ is a good source of information. Most towns have an _________, library or other computer service provider where you can access this. Use a _________ such as _________ or _________ to enter key words which will help you find the information you need. The BBC _________ (www.bbc.co.uk) is particularly recommended for news and information from around the world.

Exercise 2: In the UK there are a lot of groups and organisations that you can telephone in the event of a specific problem. These all provide free help and information on their *helplines*. Complete sentences 1 – 14 below with one of these groups from the box.

• BT Customer Services • Childline • Crimestoppers • DVLA
• Equal Opportunities Commission • HM Revenue and Customs • NHS Direct
• Parentline Plus • Refugee Council • Samaritans • Seniorline • Shelterline
• Transco • Victim Supportline

1. Mr Michaud and his family came to the UK to escape threats and persecution in their country. They want to try to get permanent residence in the UK, so Mr Michaud calls the _________ on 0207 820 3085.
2. Mr Watkins is self-employed and has some questions about paying tax. He calls _________ on 0845 010 9000.
3. Ms Ranscombe passed her driving test recently, but has not received her new, full driving licence. She calls the _________ on 0870 240 0009.
4. Mrs Taylor wants to have a telephone line installed in her house. She calls _________ on 0800 800 150, and they put her through to the correct department.
5. Alan Bradley believes that his neighbour is selling illegal drugs from her house. He reports her anonymously by calling _________ on 0800 555 111.
6. Ms Treby believes that she has been denied a job she applied for because of her age. She calls the _________ for advice on 0845 601 5901.
7. Mr Wade is a pensioner and would like some advice on the services for older people in his area. He calls _________ on 0808 800 6565.
8. Tony Sheppard has been evicted from his flat and has nowhere to live and no friends he can stay with. He calls _________ on 0808 800 4444.
9. Janet White's friend is feeling very depressed after she lost her job and her husband left her. Janet has done everything she can to cheer her friend up, but with no result, so suggests that she calls the _________ on 08457 909090.
10. Alice Walker is a single mother who is struggling to raise her two young children. She calls _________ on 0808 800 2222.
11. There is a strong smell of gas in Mrs Dowling's house. She calls _________ on 0800 111 999.
12. John Withers has very bad flu, but is unable to visit his doctor. He calls _________ on 0845 4647 and asks them what he can do to get over it more quickly.
13. Neil Jefferson, aged 15, is very unhappy and worried because he is being bullied a lot at school. He calls _________ on 0800 1111 for help and advice.
14. Mr Dyson's house has been burgled twice in the last month. On the second occasion, the burglars attacked him when he tried to stop them. Naturally he is feeling upset and vulnerable. He calls the _________ on 0845 30 30 900.

Match the two parts of the sentences below together. The sentence sections in the right-hand box are in the correct chronological order.

King Henry VII…

The Emperor Hadrian…

William Shakespeare…

Vikings from Denmark and Norway…

The *Domesday Book* (the first ever census of property values)…

Missionaries from Rome, and monks from Ireland, …

Geoffrey Chaucer...

King Alfred (known as Alfred the Great)…

King Edward II…

The first charter of rights, called *Magna Carta*, …

Elizabeth, Henry's daughter by one of his marriages,…

William Caxton…

Queen Boudicca, a Briton of the Iceni tribe, …

Jutes, Angles and Saxons…

King Henry VIII…

The Emperor Claudius…

The Spanish Armada, …

Julius Caesar…

William, the Duke of Normandy in France, …

The laws of England…

…led the Roman army on an exploratory foray into Britain in 55BC.

…led the Romans on a successful invasion of Britain, resulting in a period of Roman rule lasting for almost 400 years.

…led an unsuccessful rebellion against the Roman occupation.

…built a wall (which can still be seen) in the north of the country to protect Britain from the Celts in (what is now) Scotland.

…from Denmark and North Germany began invading the country.

…began to spread Christianity across Britain.

…invaded, and many then settled and farmed.

…of the Kingdom of Wessex united the Saxons and defeated the Danish and Viking armies.

…led the last successful invasion of Britain and defeated the Saxon King Harold at the Battle of Hastings in 1066.

…was compiled and written.

…was signed by King John after he was forced to do so by the great barons. This effectively showed that the power of the King was not absolute.

…was defeated by the Scot Robert the Bruce at the Battle of Bannockburn in 1314.

…wrote his literary masterpiece, *The Canterbury Tales*.

…started using Britain's first printing press (introduced from Germany).

…won the Battle of Bosworth, which ended the Wars of the Roses and established the Tudor dynasty. This was to rule England for 118 years and introduce some of the most profound changes to the country.

…broke from the Church of Rome and, in a period known as *the Reformation*, established the Church of England.

…began to be imposed on Wales in 1536.

…became Queen when her half-sister Queen Mary died childless. During her reign, art and literature flourished.

…a fleet of ships sent to conquer England and restore the Catholic faith in 1588, was defeated.

…wrote some of the most famous literary works in the world, including *Romeo and Juliet*, *Hamlet* and *The Merchant of Venice*.

History 2

Below you will see some of the key historical events in Britain and the United Kingdom between 1603 and 1945. Complete these with words and expressions from the box.

- Act of Union • Battle of the Boyne • Battle of Culloden • Battle of Waterloo
- Bonnie Prince Charlie • Charles II • Emancipation Act • English Civil War
- First World War • George I • House of Windsor • India • Industrial Revolution
- Ireland (x2) • Irish • James I • James VI • monarchy • Napoleon Bonaparte
- Oliver Cromwell • republic • Republic of Ireland • Scotland • slavery
- Suffragette Movement • vote • War of Independence • William of Orange
- Winston Churchill

1. ________ of Scotland became ________ of England following the death of Queen Elizabeth I in 1603.
2. King Charles I was overthrown and executed following the ________ (1642 – 1649).
3. In 1650, England became a ________, with ________ at its head.
4. In 1660, the ________ was restored, with ________ (Charles I's son) becoming king.
5. In 1688, the Protestant ________ (a part of the Netherlands) was invited to become King, replacing the Catholic James II.
6. Following William's victory against the forces of James II at the ________ in 1690, England assumed control of the whole of ________, extending their influence beyond the north of the country.
7. The Kingdoms of England and ________ were united in the ________ in 1707.
8. The Hanoverian dynasty (now called the ________) began with the reign of King ________ (a German from Hanover).
9. Charles Stuart (known as ________), the grandson of James II, led an unsuccessful rebellion against the English in Scotland. He was finally defeated at the ________ in 1745.
10. The ________ began in the middle of the 18th century, bringing enormous social and economic changes to the country.
11. Britain lost its American colonies in the American ________. Meanwhile, it was extending its colonial influence in other areas, especially in ________ (and later in Africa).
12. The French Emperor ________, who had successfully conquered much of Europe, was finally defeated at the ________ in 1815.
13. Following lengthy campaigns from people such as William Wilberforce, the ________ of 1833 finally abolished ________ throughout the British empire.
14. The Great War (now known as the ________) began in 1914, and over the next four years millions died in France and elsewhere.
15. After much agitation and campaigning by the Women's ________, women over 30 won the right to ________ in 1918. This was extended to all women aged 21 or over in 1928.
16. ________ nationalists unsuccessfully rebelled against British rule in 1916. Five years later, however, following a guerrilla war, ________ was partitioned. The south eventually became the ________, and the north-east remained part of the UK.
17. ________ led Britain in an alliance with other countries to defeat Hitler and the Nazis in the Second World War of 1939 – 1945.

Complete these sentences with the correct name, word or expression in **bold**.

1. In 1945, following the Second World War, a **Conservative / Labour / Liberal** government was elected.
2. Under Prime Minister Clement Attlee, the **National Health Service / the Common Market / the Sex Discrimination Act** was started.
3. In the period up to 1951, many institutions, including coal mines, electricity, gas and water supplies and the **railways / pubs / farms** were put under public ownership.
4. In **1953 / 1955 / 1958**, Elizabeth II was crowned Queen of the UK.
5. In the thirty years following the Second World War, the UK lost many of its overseas territories, including **Ireland / India / the USA** in 1947.
6. Countries that used to be under the political control of the UK became an organisation known as **the Empire / the League of Nations / the Commonwealth**.
7. The UK and western Europe were profoundly affected by the "**Iron Curtain**" / "**Rubber Wall**" / "**Timber Turnstile**" that divided West from East Europe following the Second World War.
8. From 1945 until the early 1970s, the UK experienced a lot of immigration, especially from the West Indies, India, Pakistan and **Bangladesh / Canada / Brazil**.
9. **Edward Heath / Harold Wilson / Winston Churchill** led the Labour government from 1964, and again briefly from 1974. This was the period when trade unions were at their most powerful and influential.
10. British industry suffered a lot during the 1960s and 1970s as a result of **a revolution / strikes / a financial crash**.
11. In 1972, the UK joined **NATO / the EEC / the UN**.
12. In 1979, **Elizabeth Windsor / Emmeline Pankhurst / Margaret Thatcher** became the first female Prime Minister of the UK.
13. The **Conservative / Labour / Liberal Party** ran the country from 1979.
14. During this period, many industries and public services were **nationalised / privatised / abolished**.
15. In **1995 / 1996 / 1997**, Tony Blair became Prime Minister with his "New Labour" government.
16. From this year onwards, many private industries that had once been under public ownership **reverted to public ownership / remained under private ownership / were forced to close down**.
17. A policy of **revolution / evolution / devolution** in the late 1990s resulted in the formation of the Welsh Assembly and the Scottish Parliament.
18. The Northern Ireland Assembly was established after various political groups fighting for control of Northern Ireland signed the **Christmas Day / Easter Monday / Good Friday** Agreement.
19. Tony Blair's government won two more general elections in **1999 and 2003 / 2000 and 2004 / 2001** and **2005**.
20. In terms of standards of living, UK citizens are now considered to be **better off than / worse off than / about the same** as they were 50 years ago.

Housing and accommodation

Fill in the gaps in this text with appropriate words, and write these in the crossword grid on the next page. The *first* and *last* letters of each word have been given to you, and these are followed by the location of that word in the crossword grid (for example, 1 ⇨ = 1 across, 13 ⇩ = 13 down, etc). Where two words are needed, there will be no gap between them in the grid.

About 66% of the UK population own or are buying their own home. The rest live in accommodation that they **r**________**t** (2 ⇩).

Most people buy their property using a **m**________**e** (23 ⇩), a special kind of loan specifically for buying property, available from banks or **b**________**g** ________**s** (14 ⇨). On average, these are paid back over 25 years. It is important that you are able to pay this money regularly, otherwise you risk losing your property to the lender.

Most property in the UK is sold through an **e**________**e a**________**y** (15 ⇩) which can be found on most high streets. If a property is for sale and you are interested in buying it, you will need to make an **a**________**t** (16 ⇨) to **v**________**w** (12 ⇨) it. If the price of a property is too high for you, it is considered acceptable to make a lower **o**________**r** (3 ⇩) to the seller. When you indicate that you want to buy a property, it is important that your offer is 'subject to **c**________**t** (27 ⇨)', which means that you can **w**________**w** (17 ⇩) from the sale for any reason before any papers are signed.

When buying a property, you should always employ the services of a good **s**________**r** (22 ⇩) to carry out a thorough **s**________**y** (1 ⇨) (to make sure that the property is in good condition, and that no **r**________**s** (8 ⇨) need to be made). It is also essential that you employ the services of a good **s**________**r** (10 ⇨), who will carry out various legal **c**________**s** (26 ⇩) on the property.

Accommodation can be rented from a local **a**________**y** (18 ⇩) (such as your local council). You will need to get your name on a **w**________**g** (24 ⇨) list known as a housing **r**________**r** (9 ⇩). This housing is allocated on a **p**________**y** (21 ⇨) basis: people with the greatest needs are **a**________**d** (25 ⇩) housing before anyone else (for example, people with young children, women who are expecting a baby, etc).

Accommodation can also be rented from housing **a**________**s** (13 ⇩). These are **i**________**t** (11 ⇩) organisations that provide accommodation for people who need it. They do not make a **p**________**t** (28 ⇨). Many offer shared-**o**________**p** (19 ⇨) schemes for people who want to own property but who cannot afford it.

A lot of property is privately owned and rented out by **l**________**s** (32 ⇨). They often run their property through a **l**________**g** (20 ⇨) agency, but many advertise their property themselves in newspapers. If you rent accommodation this way, you will be expected to sign a contract known as a **l**________**e** (33 ⇨) (also called a **t**________**y** (6 ⇨) agreement). In most cases, you will be expected to pay a **d**________**t** (4 ⇩) (usually one month's rent, which you should get back when you leave the property, provided the property and everything in it is in good condition). Rent is then normally paid monthly in **a**________**e** (7 ⇨), which means that you pay for each month you are there at the beginning of that month.

Before you agree to move into rented accommodation, you should always check a few important points: whether the accommodation is **f**________**d** (29 ⇩) (are there beds, sofas, etc already in the property?), how long the **t**________**y** (6 ⇨ again) lasts (most are for six months, with an option to extend at the end of that period), and whether or not there are any special rules (for example, many landlords specify that you cannot smoke in their property, or that you cannot have pets). If you break these rules, you could be **e**________**d** (34 ⇩) (told to leave the property).

Note that the person living in rented accommodation (the **t**________**t** (5 ⇨ *again*)) cannot be forced out of their home without being given sufficient **n**________**e** (31 ⇩) (a written note that they must leave the property). Also note that landlords cannot **d**________**e** (35 ⇩) against someone because of their sex, race, religion, etc (in other words, it is illegal to refuse someone accommodation on these grounds).

People who are unemployed or on a low income could be entitled to receive housing **b**________**t** (30 ⇨). This is money which is paid by the local authority to cover all or part of the rent.

Legal matters 1

How much do you know about law and the police in the UK? Test your knowledge with this quiz.

1. Who is responsible for setting the general standards and priorities of the police in the United Kingdom? Is it:

   (a) The Prime Minister (b) The Home Secretary (c) Local judges (d) The Lord Chancellor (e) The monarch

2. Complete this sentence with one word:

   There are 43 police __________ in England and Wales, eight in Scotland, and one in Northern Ireland.

3. Do police in the United Kingdom carry guns?
4. What telephone number should you call if you witness a crime, or if you are involved in a crime?
5. Can you report a crime using email?
6. Is it an offence for a member of the public to carry (a) a gun, and ((b) a knife in a public place?
7. The police have three main roles. Complete this paragraph with appropriate words. The first and last letter of each word have been given to you:

   The police must protect l__________e and p__________y (houses, shops, factories, cars, possessions, etc). They are also required to prevent d__________s (such as fighting in the street, hooliganism, people playing very loud music at night, etc). At the same time, they must prevent and detect c__________e.

8. If you suffer or witness police *misconduct*, can you do anything about it?
9. Can the police stop you in the street or in your vehicle at any time, and search you / your vehicle?
10. If you are stopped by the police, what information should you give them? Choose from the following options.

    (a) Your name (b) Your age (c) Your job (d) Your nationality (e) Your passport or ID number (f) Your address or place of residence (g) What you are doing (h) Where you are going

11. In return, what information can you ask from them?
12. What would happen to you if you were rude to a police officer?
13. Complete this paragraph with appropriate words. The first and last letter of each word have been given to you:

    If the police want to enter and search a building, they need a w__________t, which they obtain from a local m__________e. They do *not* need one of these if they need to get into a building to a__________t someone, to s__________e someone's life, or to prevent d__________e or d__________e.

14. Now do the same with this paragraph:

    If the police arrest you, they must give you a reason, and then c__________n you (in other words, they officially warn you that anything you say may be used as e__________e against you). If you have problems understanding English, they should provide an i__________r. You have some rights, including the right to see a s__________r (free of charge: each police station should have access to a d__________y s__________r, who advises people who have been arrested), the right to send a m__________e to someone to let them know where you are, and the right to look at the police codes of p__________e (a list of guidelines that the police must follow).

15. If you are a victim of crime, can you get compensation?

Exercise 1:
Complete definitions 1 – 30 with words / expressions from the box. Note that several of these are related to English and Welsh law only.

■ barrister	■ employment tribunal	■ magistrate
■ Citizens' Advice	■ European Court of Human Rights	■ Magistrates' Court
■ coroner's court	■ European Court of Justice	■ No win, no fee
■ coroner	■ High Court	■ rent tribunal
■ County Court	■ House of Lords	■ sentence
■ Court of Appeal	■ judge	■ small claims court
■ Crown Court	■ Jury	■ solicitor
■ CPS	■ jury service	■ suspect
■ defendant	■ lawyer	■ witness
■ dispute	■ legal aid	■ youth court

1. A __________ is a court that deals with arguments over small amounts of money (usually less than £5000).
2. A __________ is a civil or criminal court to which a person may go to ask for an award or sentence to be changed.
3. A __________ is the general name for anyone who is qualified to provide people with legal advice and services.
4. A __________ is someone who sees a crime take place.
5. A __________ is one of the types of court in England and Wales which hears local civil cases.
6. The __________ is a court which considers the rights of citizens of states which are parties to the *European Convention for the Protection of Human Rights*.
7. An __________ is a body responsible for hearing work-related complaints.
8. A __________ is a court in England and Wales where minor crimes are judged. It can also commit someone for trial or sentencing in a Crown Court.
9. A __________ is a judge in number 8 above, and also in number 25 below.
10. __________ is an organisation that gives people free advice on legal, financial and social problems.
11. A __________ is a court above the level of a Magistrates' court which hears criminal cases.
12. A __________ is a group of people (usually 12 ordinary members of public) who judge a court case in a Crown Court.
13. __________ is the obligation to be part of number 12 above, and can be done by anyone whose name is on the electoral register.
14. A __________ is a court which decides in disputes about money paid or services provided in return for leasing something – usually buildings or land.
15. The __________ is the main civil court in England and Wales.
16. The __________ is the court set up to see that the principles of law as laid out in the Treaty of Rome are observed and applied correctly in the European Union.
17. A __________ is a lawyer who gives legal advice, writes legal contracts, and represents people in the lower courts of law (for example, in a Magistrates' Court or County Court).
18. '__________' refers to cases in which the person in number 17 above only charges his / her client if they win their case.
19. A __________ is a lawyer in England or Wales who is allowed to speak in the higher law courts (for example, in the Crown Court).

20. The __________ is the highest court of appeal in the United Kingdom (although anyone who is unhappy with a decision made here can appeal to the European Court of Justice).
21. A __________ is a court presided over by a public official (usually a doctor or lawyer) who investigates sudden, unexpected and violent deaths.
22. A __________ is someone who hears a case and makes decisions in number 21 above.
23. A __________ is someone who makes decisions in a court of law (for example, in a Crown Court, he / she may send someone to prison).
24. The __________ is the official organisation in England and Wales that decides whether the police have found enough evidence to have a court case against someone.
25. A __________ is a special type of court for people under 18 who have been accused of doing something wrong.
26. A __________ is someone who the police believe may have committed a crime (it can also be a verb: *to __________ someone of something*).
27. A __________ is a punishment given by a judge, usually involving a period of time that must be spent in prison. (it can also be a verb: *to __________ someone to five years in prison*).
28. A __________ is someone who has been accused of a crime and is on trial.
29. __________ is a system in which the government pays for people to get advice about the law or be represented in court when they do not have enough money for this.
30. A __________ is a disagreement or arguments between parties.

Exercise 2:

Complete these sentences with the most appropriate word or words from exercise 1.

1. Mr Johnson and Mrs Johnson are getting divorced. Mrs Johnson demands to have the house, the car and 75% of Mr Johnson's life savings. Mr Johnson disagrees. Their case is taken up by their __________, and eventually goes to a __________ for judgement.
2. Five workers have been sacked from the energy company *Dilligas*. They believe that they have been unfairly dismissed, and so after getting advice from their local __________, they take their case to a / an __________.
3. Mr and Mrs Waugh had a new window installed in their house. The window company now wants the Waughs to pay, but Mr Waugh is refusing because he thinks the quality of workmanship is poor. The company takes them to the __________ to get their money.
4. Jamie Yarnton pays £500 a month to live in a house that belongs to Mrs Cassington. Suddenly, Mrs Cassington asks him for £1000 a month instead. Mr Yarnton thinks this is completely unreasonable. He hopes that a __________ will decide in his favour.
5. A national newspaper accuses the Prime Minister of stealing money from his own party. The PM accuses the newspaper of telling lies. The __________ is taken to the __________, where the newspaper is ordered to pay £85,000 in damages to the PM. The newspaper thinks this is unfair, and goes to a __________ to try to reduce the amount they need to pay.
6. Laurence Bailey robs a bank. The day after he is arrested, he appears in a __________ for an initial hearing. The __________ tells Mr Bailey that he will have to appear for trial in a __________. Although he hires a good __________ to represent him in court, the __________ find him guilty. The __________ decides he must be punished, and __________ him to eight years in prison.

Rearrange the letters in **bold** to make words, and write these in the crossword grid on the next page. Where two words are needed, there will be no gap between these words in the grid.

Across (⇨)

5. The **ilWedomnb** tennis championships, which are held in south London, are watched by millions of people all over the world.
6. Employees aged 16 and over are entitled to at least four weeks of paid **liyhaod** each year.
7. The **olaitnNa utrTs** is a charitable organisation that owns and looks after historical buildings and areas of countryside for people to visit.
10. If you are interested in joining a local club or society, a good source of information is your local Council or **yblirra**.
11. Local newspapers advertise details of films, plays, concerts, **teibiixnhso** and other special events.
15. Satellite, cable and digital television broadcasters usually charge viewers a fee, but there are several **wrvieefe** channels for which viewers do not need to pay anything.
18. People who treat their pets or other animals badly can be prosecuted by a national charity organisation called the RSPCA (the Royal Society for the **rnPioveten** of **rCltyue** to animals).
23. A good way of discovering places of interest in the countryside is to use the large network of public **spotofath** that cross the country.
24. For people who enjoy watching horse racing, the **nrdaG taioNnla** is one of the biggest sporting events of the year.
25. Pet owners are responsible for any **madgea** their animal causes if they know it is likely to cause such damage.
26. In the UK, entrance to many **susmemu** and **eglriesal** is free.

Down (⇩)

1. Football, rugby and **icktecr** are three sports that have a major following in the UK.
2. Public holidays in the UK are often called **aknb** holidays.
3. In many towns and cities, the consumption of **ollcaho** in public places such as the street or park is banned.
4. A television **neeiclc** is required if you own a television or a computer that can receive television programmes. These last for 12 months.
8. During school holidays, libraries and leisure centres organise special **tiacvesiti** for children.
9. The best, most detailed maps of the United Kingdom are those produced by **dennOrca uvyreS**.
12. The pub is an important institution for many people in the UK. The word 'pub' is a short form of '**culipb suhoe**'.
13. **lAtud deatucnio** courses are a good way of improving your employment skills, learning a new hobby or improving your general education.
14. Hotels in the UK can be expensive places to stay. In many cases, a **edb** and **asarebkft** (a *B and B*, also called a *guest house*) is a cheaper option. These can be found in nearly all villages, towns and cities across the country, as well as in the countryside.
16. Films and DVDs which are graded PG (**ratlenpa incdguae**) are suitable for general viewing, but some scenes may not be suitable for children unless their parents decide otherwise.

17. A lot of cinemas, theatres, etc, offer **sinsncecoso** to children, students, families and elderly people (in other words, they charge them a reduced price).
19. For football supporters, the FA **puC lnaFi** is one of the biggest sporting events of the year.
20. If you want to buy a **oltyrte** ticket or scratch card, you must be at least 16 years old.
21. The BBC is an organisation that broadcasts television and radio programmes. Unlike other broadcasters, its programmes do not have **amcmerlosci**.
22. You cannot go into a betting shop or **aignblgm** club if you are under 18.

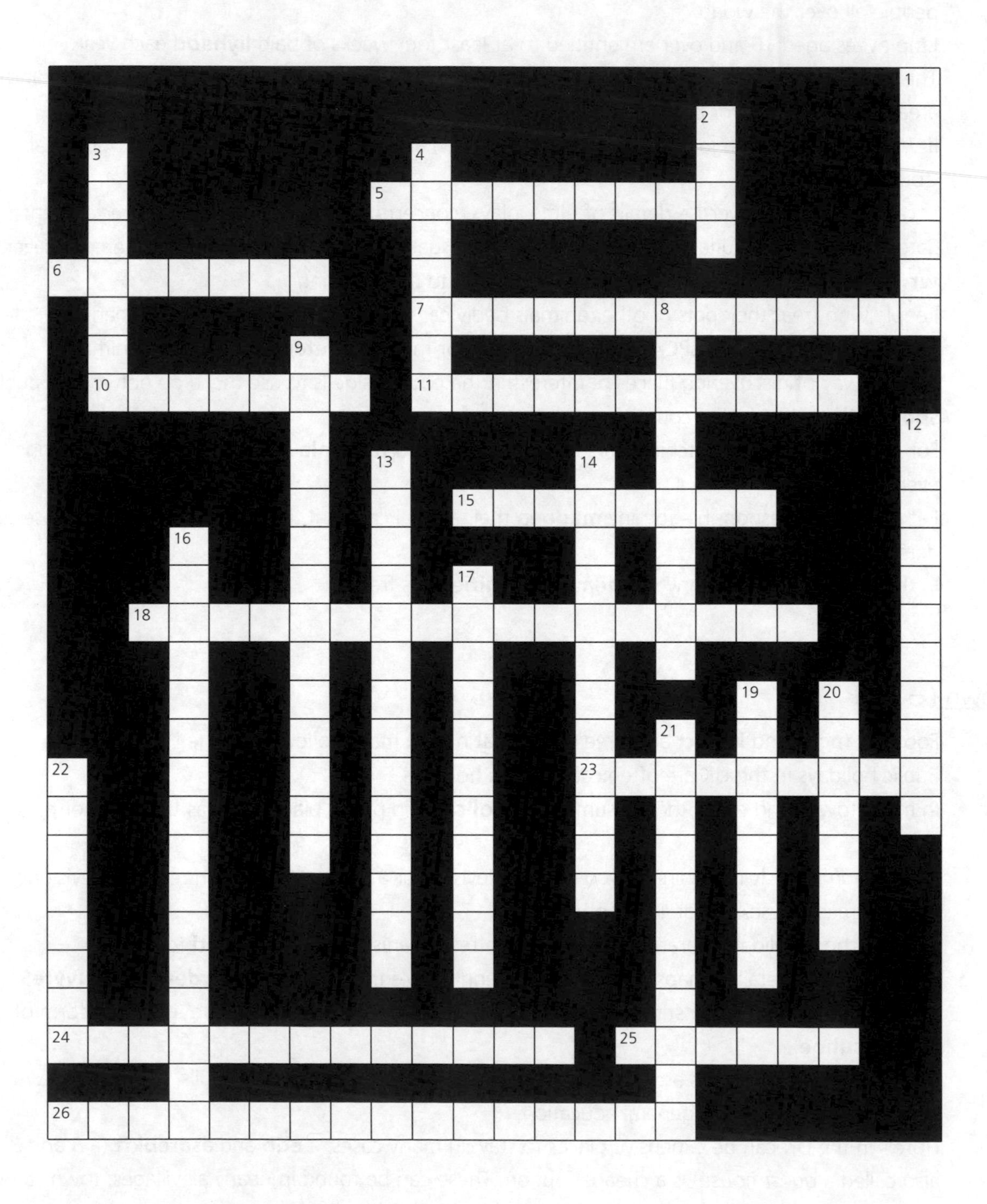

The monarchy

Before you do this exercise, you might find it helpful to look at the exercises on Politics and government on pages 36 – 42.

Look at the sentences below, and rearrange the letters in **bold** to make words.

1. Britain has a **sotntintiolacu noyharcm**, which means that the powers and rights of the King or Queen (the monarch) are limited by the basic laws and principles of the country.
2. The name of the current monarch is Queen **itaelEhzb** II, and she has **nidgree** the country since 1952.
3. Her official London residence is at **miucnBaghk ealPca**, but she has other residences around the country that she uses.
4. Her husband is called Prince **hilpPli** (the **kueD** of **bdhiurEgn**) and they have four children.
5. Their eldest child is **leCsarh** (the **iPecnr** of **lsaWe**, and the person who will eventually succeed the Queen: he is the **ehri** to the **nhrote**).
6. Her other children are Prince **redAwn** (the Duke of York), Prince **dadwEr** (the Earl of Wessex) and Princess **neAn** (known as the *Princess Royal*).
7. Collectively, they are known as the **oRlya mayiFl**, and are sometimes referred to as the **soHeu** of **nWodirs** (after their family name, which they changed from Saxe-Coburg during the First World War).
8. The monarch is the Head of State of the United Kingdom, and is also the monarch or head of state of many of the countries in the British **womenmCothal** (an organisation of countries that used to be under the political control of the UK). She is also the head of the **uhCrhc** of **nlEdgna**.
9. The monarch's limited powers and rights (see number 1 above) are known as the royal **pogtrevraie**. However, her role is one of a **egfiredhua** (a leader with no real power or influence) and is largely **mociaereln**.
10. For example, she meets and greets foreign heads of state. Each year she also opens **maenrlaPti** and gives the **sueQn'e hpesce**, in which she outlines the **ielospic** of the government for the coming year.
11. This speech does not express her views: it expresses the views of the **meriP stinirMe** and the **nlguri** political party.
12. The monarch must accept any decisions made by the **naCiteb** and by Parliament.
13. The monarch cannot voice **opsrtpu** for or **popiinosot** to the government. However, he or she can **savdei**, **anwr** and **agecouner** the government, usually at a weekly meeting with the Prime Minister.
14. Following advice from the Prime Minister, the monarch can **popinat** people to high positions in the **mogternevn**, the **uhrChc** of **nndlEag** and the **mdrae esrocf**.
15. The monarchy is still very popular in Britain, although increasing numbers of people want to remove the current system and replace it with a **pulrecbi** and an elected **deritPnes**.

Money and finance

Test your knowledge with this quiz. Use your dictionary to check the meanings of the words and expressions in *italics*, or any other words and expressions that you do not understand. Make a note of these in the box at the end of the exercise on the next page.

1. What is the official name of the *currency* used in the United Kingdom?
2. In which of the following denominations are banknotes printed?:
   (a) £1 (b) £2 (c) £5 (d) £10 (e) £15 (f) £20 (g) £25 (h) £30 (i) £50
3. Can banknotes that are printed in Scotland and Northern Ireland be used in England and Wales?
4. Is the *Euro legal tender* in the UK?
5. In what situation would *exchange rates* and *commission charges* be relevant?
6. If you want to open a bank account in the UK, what will you need to show the bank?
7. In addition to looking after your money, and lending you money, what other services can banks provide?
8. What is the difference between a *loan* and a *mortgage*?
9. What is the difference between a *bank* and a *building society*?
10. If you have a regular, full-time job, why is it important for you to have a bank account?
11. Each month, a bank sends its customers a printed record of the money they have withdrawn from, and put into, their bank account. What is this record called?
    (a) a balance (b) a credit note (c) a money order (d) a statement
12. Banks and building societies often automatically offer their customers an *overdraft facility*. What is this?
13. What is the difference between a *credit card* and a *debit card*?
14. What is the difference between a *debit card* and a *cash card*?
15. To use a cash card, debit card or credit card, you will need to know and use your *PIN*. What do you think these letters stand for?
16. Do you have to pay to use a *cash machine*?
17. Often, when using a debit card in a large store (especially in a supermarket), you will be asked if you want any *cash back*. What does this mean?
18. A major shopping chain offers you a *store card*. What is this?
19. Credit card companies in the UK are often criticised in financial reports written for consumers. Why do you think this is?
20. Before you borrow money, you should always check the *APR*. What is this?
21. If you have a savings account, you pay tax on the interest you receive. However, there is one special type of savings account in which you do not pay tax on interest. What is the name of this kind of account?
    (a) an ISA (b) an ISBN (c) an IRS (d) an ISO

22. Many people pay for household bills, and make other regular payments, using *direct debit*. What do you think this is?
23. What is the difference between a *direct debit* and a *standing order*?
24. You apply for a *loan*, but you are *refused credit*. Can you find out why?
25. Which of the following are not banks in the UK?

    (a) Waitrose (b) NatWest (c) Lloyds TSB (d) John Lewis (e) RBS (f) Barclays (g) Debenhams (h) HSBC (i) BHS (j) Asda
26. Your bank account is *in the red*. What does this mean?
27. Where would you go to open a *National Savings Account*?
28. If you shop or bank *online*, why is it important that you see a padlock symbol (similar to this: 🔒) at the bottom of your computer screen: ?
29. What do we call organisations that sell insurance on behalf of different insurance companies? Choose from the following:

    (a) breakers (b) brokers (c) braziers (d) breadwinners (e) broadcasters
30. What is *social security*?

Use this space to make a note of key words and expressions

On the road

Exercise 1: Complete paragraphs 1 – 7 with words and numbers from the box. You will need to use some of these words / numbers more than once.

3 12 17 18 21 125 Agency bus car comprehensive disqualification DVLA Driver European Union fine full garage insurance invalid learner Licensing lorry L-plates MOT motorcycle motorway penalties post office practical provisional public road tax skills tax disc taxed theory third valid Vehicle

1. You must be at least **(a)**________ years old to drive a **(b)**________ or ride a **(c)**________ on a public road. You must be at least **(d)**________ years old to drive a medium-sized **(e)**________. You must be at least **(f)**________ years old to drive a large **(g)**________ or a **(h)**________.

2. It is illegal to drive on a public road without a driving licence. It is also illegal to drive if your vehicle is not **(a)**________ (a **(b)**________ must be displayed in the windscreen of your car), and you must have **(c)**________. **(d)**________ party **(e)**________ is the minimum requirement, but many people have fully **(f)**________ **(g)**________, which covers damage to their own vehicle. The **(h)**________ for not having **(i)**________ are severe, and can include a **(j)**________ or a **(k)**________ from driving. Furthermore, if the vehicle you are driving is over **(l)**_____ years old, it must have an annual **(m)**________ test (which can be done at an approved **(n)**________) to make sure it is safe to use on the road. If your car fails this test, your **(o)**________ will become **(p)**________.

3. Before you learn to drive, you must apply for a **(a)**________ licence. This allows you to practise driving a car (or ride a **(b)**________ of **(c)**________cc or less) with someone in the front seat next to you. This person must be at least **(d)**________ years old, and must have held a **(e)**________ licence for at least **(f)**________ years. You can get an application form for a **(g)**________ licence from a **(h)**________. You can also renew your **(i)**________ there.

4. As a **(a)**________-driver, your vehicle must display **(b)**________ at the front and back, so that other road users can see you are learning. While you are learning to drive, you can drive on any **(c)**________ road except a **(d)**________.

5. To obtain a **(a)**________ licence (which allows you to drive a vehicle on your own), you must pass a written **(b)**________ test, and also pass a **(c)**________ test, which should show you have the right **(d)**________ needed to drive a vehicle safely. If you pass these tests, you will need to exchange your **(e)**________ licence for a **(f)**________ licence.

6. If you have a **(a)**________ licence and come from a **(b)**________ country, or from Iceland, Liechtenstein or Norway, you can drive a vehicle in Britain on that licence for as long as that licence is **(c)**________. If you come from a country outside the EU, you can drive on your current licence for **(d)**________ months, but after that you will need to take the test described in paragraph 5 above.

7. The British government organisation that is responsible for providing driving licences and collecting road tax is called the **(a)**________ (= the **(b)**________ and **(c)**________ **(d)**________ **(e)**________).

Exercise 2: Test your knowledge with this quiz.

1. (a) In the UK, what are road distances and speeds measured in?
   (b) What is the equivalent of this in kilometres?
2. Only the driver and front seat passenger in a car are required by law to wear seat belts. Is this *true or false*?
3. (a) What must motorcycle drivers (and their passenger) always wear?
   (b) Does this apply to everyone in the UK?
4. Unless indicated otherwise, what is the maximum speed:
   (a) In built-up areas? (b) On single carriageways (= one lane going in both directions)? (c) On dual carriageways (= two lanes going in both directions) (d) motorways?
5. What does *give way* mean?
6. People in the UK drive on the *right* side of the road. Is this *true or false*?
7. (a) A man is driving a car and talking to someone on a hand-held mobile phone. Is he breaking the law?
   (b) A woman is driving a car and talking to someone on her mobile phone. She is not holding the phone, but is speaking through a headpiece that is connected to the phone. Is *she* breaking the law?
8. What is a *Breathalyser* ™, who would use one, and when would they use it?
9. What telephone number should you call if you are involved in, or witness, a serious road accident?
10. Are you *committing an offence* if you are driving a vehicle and are involved in a *hit-and-run*?
11. If you are involved in an accident (even a *minor* one) with another vehicle, what information should you get from the other drivers involved?
12. If you are involved in an accident, what is it advisable *not* to do?
13. Someone accuses you of *tailgating*. What is this?
14. You are at a junction and you are waiting to *pull out* onto a busy road. A driver on this road lets you pull out in front of him / her. What should you do?
15. You are driving along a narrow road that is just wide enough for one car. Another car is coming towards you. He / she quickly *flashes his headlights*. Is he / she:
    (a) Saying that he / she is claiming *right of way*, and you should stop and wait for him / her to pass? *or* (b) Saying that he / she is stopping his / her car to let you have right of way?
16. When should you use your *horn*?
17. You are driving your car and arrive at a *zebra crossing* (= black and white stripes painted across the road, with an orange light at each end). A pedestrian is waiting here to cross the road. Do you have to stop?
18. Rearrange these letters to make words and expressions connected with vehicles and driving. The first letter of each word is in **bold**:
    (a) p**s**endieg (b) dy**j**riiogn (c) ayisq**d**lifu (d) ta**o**veker (e) seee**r**rv (f) d**i**nitcea (g) ak**b**er
    (h) unud**r**obota (i) cfra**t**fi (hs**l**itg j) sedaentri**p** gssino**c**r (k) unni**j**oct (l) dossrosa**c**r
    (m) dpe**s**e marea**c** (n) cfra**t**fi ngli**c**am

UK places, people and institutions

Exercise 1: Test your knowledge of places, institutions, etc, in the UK. Write the words from the box in the appropriate section of the table below.

Aberdeen Aberystwyth Armagh Belfast Birmingham Bristol Cardiff Clyde Cornwall Dartmoor Edinburgh Glasgow Inverness Kent The Lake District Liverpool Londonderry Neagh Ness Newport Northumberland The North York Moors Omagh Oxfordshire Pembrokeshire Coast Severn Swansea Thames Tyne Ullswater Windermere York

Towns and cities in England	Towns and cities in Wales	Towns and cities in Scotland	Towns and cities in Northern Ireland
1. ________	1. ________	1. ________	1. ________
2. ________	2. ________	2. ________	2. ________
3. ________	3. ________	3. ________	3. ________
4. ________	4. ________	4. ________	4. ________

Counties	Rivers	National parks	Lakes
1. ________	1. ________	1. ________	1. ________
2. ________	2. ________	2. ________	2. ________
3. ________	3. ________	3. ________	3. ________
4. ________	4. ________	4. ________	4. ________

Exercise 2: Instructions as above.

Asda Ashmolean Ask Barclays Beefeater BHS BMIbaby British Airways Debenhams Dover Easyjet Gatwick Harvester Harwich Heathrow HSBC Hunterian John Lewis Little Chef Liverpool Lloyds TSB Luton Marks and Spencer Morrison's NatWest Sainsbury Southampton Stansted Tate Modern Tesco Victoria and Albert Virgin Atlantic

Banks	Supermarkets	Department stores	Places to eat
1. ________	1. ________	1. ________	1. ________
2. ________	2. ________	2. ________	2. ________
3. ________	3. ________	3. ________	3. ________
4. ________	4. ________	4. ________	4. ________

Airlines	London airports	British seaports	Museums & galleries
1. ________	1. ________	1. ________	1. ________
2. ________	2. ________	2. ________	2. ________
3. ________	3. ________	3. ________	3. ________
4. ________	4. ________	4. ________	4. ________

Exercise 3: Instructions as above.

The Ashes   Boxing Day   Canterbury Cathedral   Easter Monday   Edinburgh Castle
The FA Cup Final   The first Monday in May   The Grand National   The Guardian
Guy Fawkes Night   The Independent   Mothering Sunday   Newmarket   New Year's Day   Oxfam
The Queen's Head   The Red Cross   Remembrance Day   The Royal Regatta
The Red Lion   The Rose and Crown   The RSPCA   Saint Valentine's Day
Save the Children   Silverstone   Stonehenge   The Sun   The Telegraph
The Tower of London   Wembley Stadium   The White Hart   Wimbledon

Newspapers	Sporting events	Sporting Venues	National Holidays
1. ______	1. ______	1. ______	1. ______
2. ______	2. ______	2. ______	2. ______
3. ______	3. ______	3. ______	3. ______
4. ______	4. ______	4. ______	4. ______

Traditional days	Charity organisations	Famous tourist sights	Common pub names
1. ______	1. ______	1. ______	1. ______
2. ______	2. ______	2. ______	2. ______
3. ______	3. ______	3. ______	3. ______
4. ______	4. ______	4. ______	4. ______

Exercise 4: Instructions as above.

Benjamin Britten   The Chancellor of the Exchequer   Charles Darwin   Charles Dickens
Christianity   Conservative   Coronation Street   David Lloyd George   Eastenders   Edward Elgar
The Foreign Secretary   George Orwell   Graham Greene   Green   The Home Secretary
Isaac Newton   Islam   Hinduism   J.K.Rowling   John Constable   Judaism   Labour
The Leader of the Opposition   Liberal Democrat   Margaret Thatcher
Michael Faraday   Newsnight   Panorama   Tim Berners-Lee   Tony Blair
JMW Turner   Winston Churchill

Political parties	Government positions	Prime Ministers	Scientists & inventors
1. ______	1. ______	1. ______	1. ______
2. ______	2. ______	2. ______	2. ______
3. ______	3. ______	3. ______	3. ______
4. ______	4. ______	4. ______	4. ______

Main religions	Famous writers	Famous writers	Television programmes
1. ______	1. ______	1. ______	1. ______
2. ______	2. ______	2. ______	2. ______
3. ______	3. ______	3. ______	3. ______
4. ______	4. ______	4. ______	4. ______

Politics and government 1

How much do you know about the British political system? This exercise, and the one on page 39, will help you to test your knowledge.

In this exercise, you need to rearrange the letters in **bold** to make words, and use these words to complete the crossword on the third page. Where two or more words are needed, there will be no gap between the words in the crossword grid. In many cases you will need to cross-refer to other sentences.

Across (⇨)

2. The **oemH efiOfc** is the government department that is responsible for justice and the police.
5. The **soHeu** of **dLsro** is the part of Parliament that consists of politicians who are not elected by the people. Its main role is to examine laws that are proposed by the *34 across*.
8. The ruling political party is elected by a system known as "**rftis spat het stop**", which means that it becomes the ruling party if it wins more seats in the *34 across*, and not because it has gained more votes overall than any other party.
10. If someone is allowed to vote in a *26 across*, we say that they are **gelliebi** to vote.
12. The person who is represented by a *20 across* and who lives in a *15 down* is called a **stuntetconi**.
13. Laws, or sets of laws, are called **gitlisnloea**.
20. A **beemrM** of **maelinPrat** (an MP) is someone who people have elected to represent them in Parliament.
21. People who vote in a *26 across* are known collectively as the **treecoatel**.
22. When *20 across* (plural) ask questions of the ruling party ministers in the *34 across*, this is called **sQuotine meTi**.
24. When politicians and their assistants provide information which makes their actions seem better than they really are, this is called **nisp**.
26. People elect (= *choose*) the politicians who will govern them in a **rageeln tineelco**, which is held every five years.
29. The leader of *2 across* is called the **mHeo cryarSeet**.
30. The **binetCa** is a group of senior politicians from the ruling party chosen by the *16 down* to decide government policy.
31. The **daSowh bCitnea** is a group of senior politicians from the second largest political party in the *34 across*.
33. The **peaerkS** is the person in the *34 across* who is in charge of political debates.
34. The **sHeuo** of **mosmCon** is the part of Parliament that consists of politicians who have been elected (= *chosen*) by the people of Britain, and is the centre of political debate.
35. The three largest political parties in Britain are Labour, Conservative, and the **liarLeb metocrsaD**.

Down (⇨):

1. Many people want to change the *8 across* system, and replace it with one of **oppotilrorna** representation, where the number of seats that a political party wins in Parliament is based on the number of votes they win overall.
3. The second largest political party in the *34 across* is called the **popitinsoo**.
4. Scotland has its own Parliament, called the Parliament of Scotland, which is also known as the **tichtsSo** Parliament.
6. The government department that deals with Britain's relations with other countries is called the **noreFig ecfOfi**.
7. The head of the second largest political party in the *34 across* is called the **deaLer** of the **stOpnopioi**.
9. The British system of government is a parliamentary **madeyrocc**, which means that the people of Britain choose the politicians who will govern them.
11. The *16 down* has his / her official residence at number 10 **wingDon treSte**, in London.
14. The **oracelChln** of the **qxcreEueh** is the member of the government who is responsible for taxes and for deciding how the government spends its money.
15. The area that is represented by a *20 across* is called a **stcueoncyitn**.
16. The **meriP itnMiser** (the PM) is the leader of the political party that is in power.
17. The **reniFog ercStayre** is the British government minister who is responsible for Britain's relations with other countries.
18. When people vote, they do so by **ectser tallob**, which means that their political choice is done privately, without anyone else knowing who they have voted for.
19. A **yb-toelcine** is held to elect someone in a particular area to Parliament, usually to replace someone who has died or left the job.
23. A *16 down* can be removed by his / her party at any time if, for example, he / she loses the **eficoenncd** of his / her party.
25. The British **ustcnitoonti** is unwritten, which means that there are no written rules that state how the country is governed.
27. The street in London where the government works and where many of the government departments are based, is called **hathWlile**.
28. A **phiw** is a member of a political party whose job is to make sure that other members go where they are needed and that they vote in the correct way.
32. Wales has some independence from Parliament in London, and this power is exercised through the National **lemysAbs** for Wales.

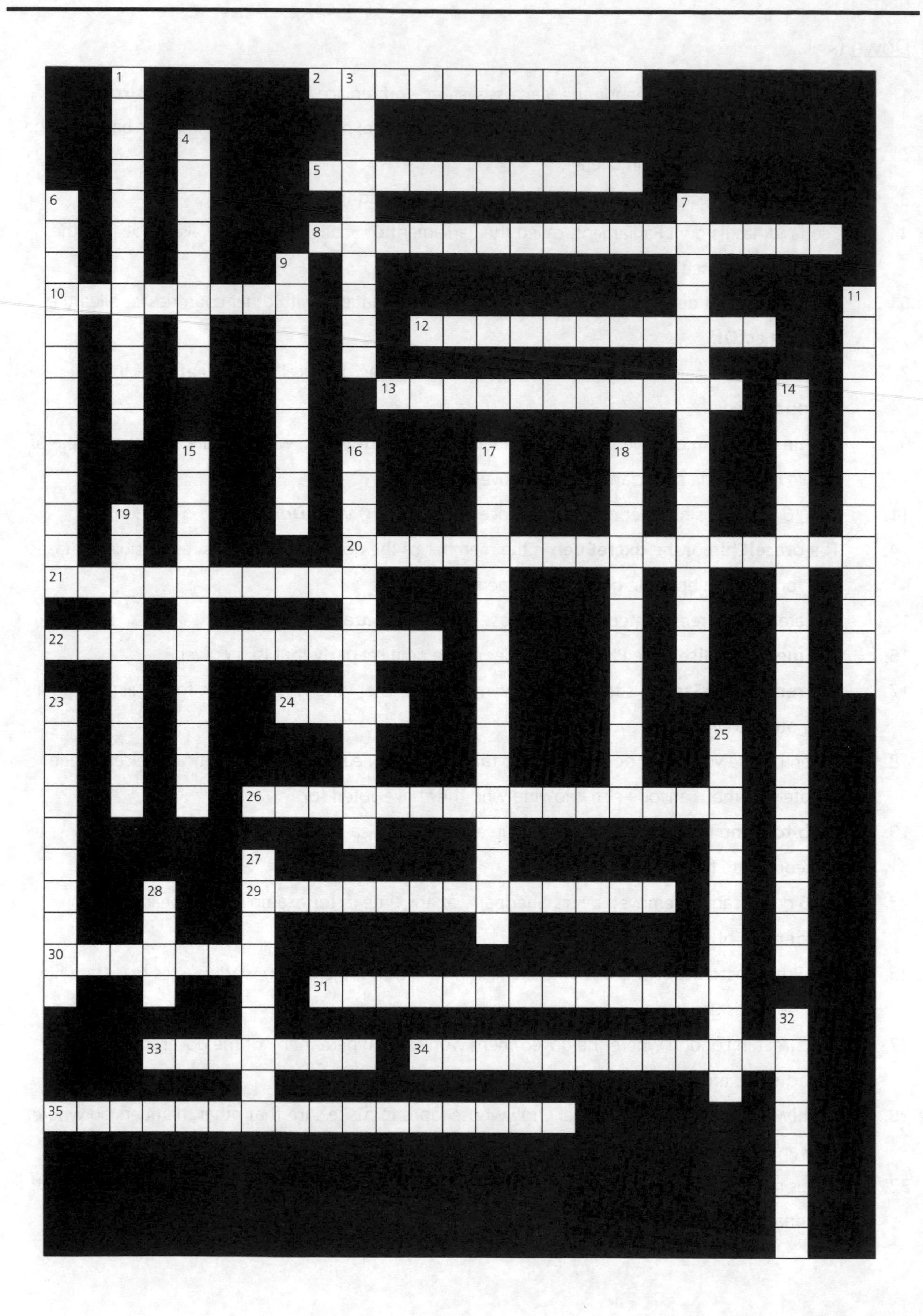

Test your knowledge with this quiz. Choose the best answer from the list of options. In some cases, more than one option may be possible.

1. What is another name for an "interest group" (an industrial, commercial, professional, financial, etc, group that tries to influence government policy?
(a) A pressure group (b) A lobby (c) A political party (d) The judiciary

2. Which of these things is a judge not allowed to do?
(a) Interpret government law (b) Decide if a law contravenes our human rights (c) Create or change a law by the decisions they make in particular cases (d) Challenge the legality of a law passed by Parliament

3. Judgements in law are usually based on previous similar cases What must a judge do, however, if there has not been a similar case to the one he / she is judging?
(a) Make his / her own judgement (b) Ask Parliament to make the judgement for him / her (c) Apply to the Queen for a judgement (d) Cancel the case

4. Who appoints judges to their post?
(a) The Chancellor of the Exchequer (b) The Queen (c) The Lord Chancellor (d) The Prime Minister (e) The Cabinet (f) The House of Lords

5. What are the main criticisms concerning the current judiciary?
(a) The selection process for judges is not 'transparent' enough to the public (b) Judges are not representative of the general community (c) There are not enough female judges (d) There are not enough judges from ethnic minorities (e) Judges are usually only selected from a particular section of society (ie, upper-middle class) (f) Many judges are 'out of touch' with the people they judge

6. Most counties and administrative areas have their own police force The largest police force in the UK is based at *New Scotland Yard* in London. What is its name?
(a) The Thames Valley Police (b) The Special Constabulary (c) The Thought Police (d) The Metropolitan Police (e) The Chief Constable

7. Who 'controls' this police force and tells it what to do?
(a) The Government (b) Local councillors (c) Local magistrates (d) The Home Secretary (e) The Queen (f) The Prime Minister

8. Who should you contact if you have a complaint against the police?
(a) The IPCC (b) The RSPCA (c) The NSPCC (d) The DVLA (e) The C of E

9. What do we call the independent managers and administrators who carry out government policy?
(a) The Department of Social Security (b)The Family Planning Association (c) Citizens' Advice (d) The Civil Service

10. What are the two key features of this organisation?
(a) Professionalism (b) Political allegiance to the ruling political party (c) The ability to change government policy if it disagrees with it (d) Political neutrality (e) Choosing which aspects of government policy it wants to put into practice

11. What happens to this organisation if a new government is elected?
(a) It must put the new government's policies into practice (b) It is disbanded, and new managers and administrators are chosen (c) The managers and administrators continue working with the previous government for up to five years and are then 'retired'

12. Individual areas in the UK are administered by a system of local government, called *councils*. What are the main types of council?
(a) County council (b) District council (c) Borough council (d) City council (e) Metropolitan council

13. What is another name commonly used for local government?
(a) Local authorities (b) Local commands (c) Local controllers (d) Local dictators

14. What sort of community services do councils provide?
(a) Education (b) Local / regional planning (c) Public transport (d) Road maintenance (e) Recycling (f) Refuse collection (g) Libraries (h) Housing and accommodation (i) The Fire Service (j) Social services

15. What do we call a member of a local council?
(a) A counsellor (b) A councillor (c) A counciller (d) A councilor

16. How does somebody become a member of a local council?
(a) They must apply for the post, like any other job (b) They must be elected in local elections (c) They are appointed by Parliament in London (d) They must make a financial donation to the council: the biggest donation "wins"

17. What are "mandatory services"?
(a) Local government services that must be provided because the central government says they must be provided (b) Local services that a local government can provide if it wants to and has the money to do so (c) Local services that are decided by central government, but that local government can refuse to provide (d) Local services that must be provided because the people who live in that area demand them

18. Who provides the money for local government?
(a) The government (through taxes) (b) Local businesses (through voluntary donations) (c) Local people (through council tax) (d) The European Parliament (through a central European funding system)

19. Who is eligible to vote in local and national elections?
(a) Men over 18 and women over 21 (b) Men and women over 16 (c) Men and women over 18 (d) Men and women over 21 (e) Men over 18, and women over 18 if they are married (f) Men only

20. If you are a permanent resident of the UK, but are not a UK citizen, which two rights do you *not* have?
(a) A general right to vote (b) The right to free medical treatment on the NHS (c) The right to claim social security if you are unemployed (d) The right to get married to a UK citizen (e) The right to hold a British passport (f) Employment rights such as paid holidays and the minimum wage (g) The right to be represented by a Member of Parliament

21. How much money do you need to deposit if you want to stand for political office in the UK?
(a) £5000 for MP's and members of the Scottish Parliament and Welsh and Northern Ireland Assemblies, and £500 for Members of the European Parliament (b) £500 for MPs and members of the Scottish Parliament and Welsh and Northern Ireland Assemblies, and £5000 for Members of the European Parliament (c) 10% of your annual income (d) Nothing, if you are unemployed (e) Nothing, but you are not allowed to vote for yourself

22. When you make a deposit to stand for political office, what percentage of the vote must you win to get your deposit back?
(a) You don't need to win any votes (b) At least 5% (c) At least 10% (d) At least 20% (e) At least 25%

23. If you want to contact your Member of Parliament (MP), how should you do it?
(a) By writing to their constituency office (b) By writing to them at their office in the House of Commons (c) By phoning their constituency office (d) By phoning their office in the House of Commons (e) At regular 'surgeries' where the MP will be present to answer your questions (f) By email, through the website *www.writetothem.com*

24. In recent years, has the number of people voting in local and national elections:
(a) fallen? (b) risen? (c) stayed the same?

Politics and government 3

This text, which is about devolving power in UK politics, contains 50 spelling errors or wrong words. Can you identify and correct them all?

The process of taking power from a central autority or goverment and giving it to smaller, more local regions is called devalution. This began in the UK in 1997, with the result that since 1999 there has been an Assembly in Whales and a Parliament in Scottland.

The Welsh Assembly and the Scottish Parliament have control over many local issues, but can only debite the policy and laws governing general taxattion, social seccurity, defense and foreign affaires (which are decided by central government in London).

The Scottish Parliament is based in Edingburgh (Scotland's principle city), and is funded by a grunt from the UK government. Scotland has had some limited autonamy from London for quite a long time, but the decision to begin creating a seperate Parliament did not happen until a national refferendum in 1997. Unlike the Welsh Assembly (see the paragraph below), the Scottish Parliament can make its own laws (with exceptions such as those listed in the paragraph above), and even has some powers over national income tax rats. Also, unlike the Welsh Assembly and the UK Parliament, members (known as *MSPs*) are elected by a type of preportional reprasentation.

The Welsh Assembly is based in Cadiff (the Welsh capitol). Assembly members are chosen in ellections which are held every four years. It makes its own decisions on many local issues and policys such as edducation, health services and the enviroment. Although the Assembly cannot make laws for Wales, it is able to prepose laws to central UK Parliament in Westminister, who can then discuss them and possibly create legislateion based on those preposals.

The Northern Ireland Assembly, based at Stormont in Bellfast, was formed after the two main organiseations responsible for terrorist activity in the region (the *IRA* – the Irish Republiccan Army – and the *UDA* – the Ulster Defence Asociation) agreed to cease armed hostilities. In the *Good Friday Agreement* of 1998, the main political wings of these groups agreed to work together with other political parties in a power-shareing agreement which resulted in the formation of the Assembly. Its powers are similar to the Welsh Assembly. However, it can be (and occasionally has been) suspected by the central UK government if the political leaders fail to work together, or if they act against the interests of the citisens of Northern Ireland.

For most people in the UK, contact and dealings with the government are through organisations known as non-deportmental public bodies. These include: spending agencies such as regional healthy authorities and higher education founding counsels; trading bodies to raise revenu, such as *National Shavings and Investments* and the *Forestry Commision*; quasi-judical and prosecuting bodies, such as the *Monopelies and Mergers Commission*, the *Crown Prosecution Service* and the *IPCC* (see Politics and Government 2 on page 39); Statutory Advisery Bodies to Ministers, such as the *Health and Safety Commission*, the *Equal Opportunnities Commission* and the *Commission for Racist Equality*; development agencies, such as the *Highlands and Icelands Development Bored* in Scotland, and the *Welsh Development Agency*.

In the pub

Pubs are an important institution in the UK. They are places where we go to relax, meet our friends, and of course drink. Many pubs also serve food. In many smaller towns and villages they are a central feature of the community and its activities.

Test (and develop) your knowledge of pubs with this quiz.

1. *Pub* is a shortened form of which two words?
2. Pubs must be *licensed*. What does this mean?
3. Who is the *landlord* or *landlady* of a pub?
4. Some pubs have the words *free house* on a sign outside. What does this mean?
5. How old must you be to buy an alcoholic drink in a pub?
6. Are children under 16 allowed to go into pubs?
7. Can you smoke in pubs?
8. In a pub, do you sit at your table to wait to be served, or do you go directly to the bar?
9. What are *bitter*, *lager* and *stout*? What is *cider*? What are *spirits*?
10. What measurements are bitter, lager, stout and cider sold in?
11. You order a *single* whisky for yourself and a *double* brandy for your friend: how much (in *millilitres*) is each drink worth in quantity?
12. Can you buy non-alcoholic drinks in a pub?
13. What are you doing if you are *buying a round*?
14. You are in the pub with a large group of friends, and one of them suggests *starting a kitty*. What does he / she want to do?
15. Do you pay for drinks as you buy them, or do you pay for everything you have bought when you leave the pub?
16. You ask the bar person if you can *start a tab*. What do you want to do?
17. Once you have bought a drink, is there a time limit within which you have to drink it?
18. Is it normal to *tip* the people working behind the bar?
19. British people consider it very important to *queue* (for example, in a shop, at the bus stop, etc). Do they do this in a pub?
20. You are standing at the bar to buy a drink. The bar is very busy. What should you do to get the bar person's attention?
21. If you accidentally spill someone's drink, what should you do?
22. Is it considered normal or acceptable in a pub to *share* a table with people you do not know?
23. Is it considered normal or acceptable to start a conversation with a stranger in a pub?
24. Another (male) customer asks you if you know where the *gents* are. What does he want?
25. What is *pub grub*? What are *bar snacks*?
26. *Gastropubs* are becoming increasingly popular in the UK. What are they?
27. You are enjoying a drink when the bar person shouts "*Last orders!*". What does he / she mean?
28. Ten minutes later, he / she shouts "*Time please!*", and / or rings a bell. What does this mean?
29. By law, at what time do most pubs have to stop serving alcohol?
30. Can you buy alcohol in a pub to take home with you?
31. What are *darts*, *billiards*, *dominoes* and *skittles*?
32. A bar person tells you that you are *barred*. What must you do?
33. Can a bar person refuse to serve you a drink without giving you a reason?
34. *Binge drinking* is becoming a big problem in the UK. What is this?

Relationships 1: Marriage and related issues

Test your knowledge with this quiz.

1. True or false?: A contract between a man and a woman to become husband and wife is called an *engagement*.
2. When a couple become engaged, are they legally bound to marry each other?
3. In the UK, what is the minimum age for getting married (a) with your parents' written permission, and (b) *without* permission from your parents.
4. Are you allowed to marry your cousin in the UK?
5. Are *arranged marriages* legal in the UK?
6. Rearrange the letters in bold to make a word meaning *husband* or *wife*: **pusoes**
7. *True or false*?: If you have a partner, you are assumed to be married.
8. What is the *age of consent* in the UK?
9. Is *homosexuality* a crime in the UK?
10. Are *same-sex marriages* legal in Britain?
11. Are *bigamy* or *polygamy* legal in the UK?
12. What do a couple need to obtain before they can be legally married?
13. When a woman marries, must she take her husband's *surname*?
14. Do couples who marry in a *civil ceremony* have the same rights and responsibilities as those who get married in a *religious ceremony*?
15. Rearrange the letters in **bold** to make words for the places where a couple can get married: (a) a registered place of **oseligriu hwprsoi** (b) a **griteysr cfioef** (c) premises that have been approved by the **acllo tyutoarih**
16. Do *unmarried* couples who live together have the same legal rights as those who are married?
17. What is the difference between a *separation* and a *divorce*?
18. Can a woman in the UK divorce her husband?
19. A couple get married, but very soon afterwards they decide that the marriage has *irretrievably broken down* (it is not working, and will not work). How long must they wait before they can get divorced?
20. A married man wants to have children, but his wife refuses to have any. Can the man divorce his wife?
21. Is *domestic violence* a crime in the UK?
22. If a man has sex with his wife against her will, can he be accused of *rape*?

Also see Relationships 2 on the next page.

Relationships 2: Children and related issues

Test your knowledge with this quiz.

1. If an unmarried couple have children, who has *parental responsibility* for them?
   (a) The father (b) The mother (c) Both of them
2. How long does parental responsibility last?
   (a) Until the child is 16 (b) Until the child is 18 (c) Until the child is 21 (d) Until the parent(s) decide(s) that the child is old enough to look after him / herself
3. If an unmarried couple have children, who has the legal responsibility to maintain the children financially?
   (a) The father (b) The mother (c) Both of them
4. If a married couple gets divorced, who gets *custody* of their children?
5. Is a parent allowed to *smack* his / her child?
6. Does a local authority have the legal right to remove a child from its home if necessary?
7. If a divorced couple have children, one of them may be required to make regular payments to their ex-husband / ex-wife to help pay for the upbringing of the children. What are these payments called?
   (a) child support (b) child maintenance (c) child benefit (d) child pensions
8. An *unmarried* couple with two children separate. The father moves away to another town. Is he legally obliged to make payments to his ex-partner for the upbringing of the children?
9. In England and Wales, the agency responsible for the assessment, review, collection and enforcement of child payments is called the *CSA*. What do you think these letters stand for?
10. How old should children be before a CSA *ruling* no longer applies?
    (a) 15 (b) 16 (c) 17 (d) 18
11. A 16-year-old child is told by a hospital that he / she needs an operation. Does the hospital need the consent of the child's parents before the operation can take place?
12. Can a doctor or nurse provide *contraceptive* advice and treatment to someone under the age of 16?
13. The parents of a 14-year-old child go away for a short holiday, leaving the child alone in the house. Are they breaking the law?
14. A couple's 14-year-old child has a morning paper round. He starts this round at 6 o'clock in the morning. Is this legal?
15. The same couple's 13-year-old daughter has a part-time job cooking breakfasts in a café. She starts this job at 7 o'clock in the morning, and finishes at 8.30. She then goes to school. Is this legal?
16. A couple own a small shop that sells cigarettes and alcohol. They sometimes let their 15-year-old daughter serve customers. Is this legal?
17. A man lets his 16-year-old son smoke. Is he breaking the law?
18. A 17-year-old person tells his parents that he wants to learn to drive a car. Their parents tell him that it is illegal to drive a car if you are under 18. Are they correct?

Exercise 1:
Chain-stores are groups of shops that belong to the same person or company. These can be found on nearly all UK high streets (= main / most important shopping streets).

Match the names of some of the most common chain-stores in the box with their description from numbers 1 – 20.

Argos... Barclays... Boots... Cargo... Clarks... Dixons... Hallmark... HMV... Holland and Barrett... Marks and Spencer... Prêt a Manger... Next... Robert Dyas... Specsavers... Starbucks... Tesco... The Link... Thomas Cook... Waterstones... W.H.Smith...

1. ...is one of the biggest bookshop chains in the UK.
2. ...only sells mobile phones, mobile phone contracts and mobile phone accessories.
3. ... mainly sells beauty products, toiletries and medicines.
4. ... is a department store that mainly sells clothes, but is also popular for its range of high-quality food.
5. ...specialise in health foods.
6. ...is the place to go for greetings cards and small gifts.
7. ...sells kitchen, household and garden products and furniture.
8. ...is well-known mainly for its men's and women's clothes and clothing accessories.
9. ...mainly sells stationery, greetings cards, books, magazines and newspapers.
10. ...only sells shoes and shoe-related products.
11. ...sells delicious sandwiches and non-alcoholic drinks (usually to take away).
12. ...is one of several high street coffee shops.
13. ...is a shop that sells electronic equipment, especially music systems, televisions, computers and cameras.
14. ...is one of the UK's best hardware stores.
15. ...is the place you should go for glasses and contact lenses.
16. ...sells mainly CD's, DVD's and computer games.
17. ...is a good place to go to book a trip or holiday, or buy and sell foreign currency.
18. ...is one of the biggest supermarket chains in the UK.
19. ...is a shop where you order goods from a catalogue, pay for them, and collect them from a counter in the shop.
20. ...is one of the biggest bank chains in the UK.

Exercise 2:
Many countries have legislation in place to protect the rights of consumers. In the United Kingdom they are protected by laws such as the *Sale of Goods Act*, the *Supply of Goods and Services Act*, the *Distance Selling Regulations*, the *Consumer Protection Act* and the *Consumer Credit Act*.

On the next page you will see a summary of some of the key points from these laws, and some other information which consumers might find useful. Complete the paragraphs with words and expressions from the box.

• accurate description • as described • claim for compensation • cooling-off period
• credit card fraud • credit voucher • defective • delivery arrangements
• fit for intended purpose • give a refund • guarantee or warranty • opt out of
• poor workmanship • proof of purchase • reasonable care and skill
• reasonable charge • receipt • responsibilities and liabilities • satisfactory quality
• specified period • unsolicited mail • unsolicited telemarketing • wear and tear
• within a reasonable time • written confirmation

1. Providers of goods and services (including credit providers and hire companies) all have ____________ towards the customer which are aimed at protecting the customer and his / her rights.
2. When you buy goods, they must be of ____________: the condition they are in should match your expectations based on the price you paid. They should also be '____________' (in other words, they must match the description made by the provider and / or the manufacturer), and they must be '____________' (they should do what you expect them to do).
3. All goods must carry a ____________ in case they go wrong or do not meet your expectations.
4. If you need to return goods to a shop or other supplier, you should do so ____________: many shops and suppliers specify their own limit, usually 28 days, and can refuse to do anything if there is evidence of unreasonable ____________ (signs that the goods have been used more than is normal or for a purpose for which they were not designed).
5. If you take goods back to a shop, they are entitled to ask for ____________, such as a ____________, a credit card slip, etc, that shows you actually bought the goods from them.
6. Many shops may refuse (illegally, if the product you have bought is faulty or ____________) to ____________, and instead of returning your money will offer you a ____________ to use in that shop at a later date.
7. Where certain goods or services are ordered on the Internet, on-line shops should offer their customers a ____________ after they have ordered them, in case the customer decides to suddenly cancel their order.
8. On-line (Internet) shops should give the customer an ____________ of the goods being sold, and clearly state the price, ____________ and options (how and when the customer can expect to receive their goods, whether there is an extra charge for postage, et(c).
9. On-line shops should also protect customers against ____________, and should allow customers to ____________ receiving further information and ____________, ____________ or unsolicited emails. They should also send the customer ____________ of their order (often in the form of an email sent after the order has been placed).
10. If a service is being provided (for example, a mobile phone contract), and there is a ____________ for the contract, this must be clearly stated by the provider.
11. If you buy faulty goods with a credit card, and those goods cost between £100 and £300, you have an equal ____________ against the seller of the goods and the credit card company.
12. Where a service such as the repair of a car is being provided, it should be done with ____________ (an unsatisfactory standard of work or general ____________ should not be accepted by the customer) for a ____________ (the customer should not have to pay an excessive amount of money) and within a reasonable time.

Signs and notices

Where would you expect to see signs and notices 1 – 48? Choose from the most appropriate option from the box. In some cases, more than one answer may be possible.

At a bus stop. At the zoo. By the side of the road. In a bank. In a café. In a car park. In a hotel. In a pub. In a public area such as a shopping centre or park. In a shop. In a library or a hospital. In a supermarket. On the emergency alarm on a train. On a bus. On or outside a commercial or residential building. On a fire alarm. On a machine or a toilet door. On the back of a lorry or commercial vehicle. On an envelope or parcel. On the London Underground On the packet or bottle of a pharmaceutical product. On a shop window. On a wall or other empty surface. On your car windscreen. At the entrance to a toilet. In the entrance to a museum, cinema or theatre. Outside a hotel or guest house. Outside a piece of private land. Outside a pub.

1. Exact fare please.

2. Please wait here until a cashier is available.

3. Baskets only.

4. No vacancies.

5. No waiting at any time.

6. To let.

7. Pay and display.

8. For external use only.

9. Please keep clear. Gates in constant use.

10. Sunday and bank holiday: no service.

11. Trespassers will be prosecuted.

12. Silence please.

13. Out of order.

14. All major cards accepted.

15. Sale.

16. Please handle with care.

17. Please take a ticket and wait for your number to appear.

18. Ladies.

19. Gents.

20. Do not exceed the stated dosage.

21. In case of emergency, break glass.

22. No skateboarding. No ball games.

23. Fixed penalty notice.

24. No billposting.

25. B&B.

26. Fine for improper use: £50.

27. Wet paint.

28. No littering.

29. Fragile.

30. Kill your speed.

31. Stand on the right.

32. Give way.

33. Queue this side.

34. Latest checkout time: 11.00.

35. Please order food at the bar.

36. Do not feed the animals.

37. Concessions: OAPs / Students / Children under 12: £2.50.

38. Shoplifters will be prosecuted.

39. Bar open to non-residents.

40. Pool. Sky Sports. Big Screen TV.

41. Pedestrian zone.

42. Beer garden. Fine wines and ales.

43. Please buy ticket from the driver.

44. No return within 1 hour.

45. Proof of ID may be required if you appear to be under 18.

46. The management reserves the right of admission.

47. Self-service.

48. How's my driving?

This exercise tests your knowledge of some common spoken responses. In each case, choose the most appropriate word in **bold** to complete the second sentence in each sentence pair. In one case, either word is possible.

1. "How are you?"
   "I'm very **fine / well**, thanks."
2. "How are you?"
   "I'm a bit under the **clouds / weather** today."
3. "How are you feeling?"
   "To tell you the **truth / honesty**, I'm not feeling so good at the moment."
4. (*In a shop*) "Can I help you?"
   "No thanks. I'm just **looking / watching**."
5. "My pet hamster died last night."
   "Oh dear, I am **sorry / apologetic**."
6. "Aaachoooooo!"
   "**Love / Bless** you!"
7. "What are you going to get me for my birthday?"
   "Aha! Wait and **look / see**."
8. "I'm sorry I broke your pen."
   "Oh, don't **worry / fear** about it. I was going to get a new one anyway."
9. "I've just won £10,000 on the lottery."
   "No way! You're pulling my **arm / leg**!"
10. "Have a nice weekend."
    "The same **to / for** you."
11. "Hello, John."
    "Sue, hi. Come in. Make yourself at **house / home**."
12. "Please don't tell anyone what I've just told you."
    "Don't worry. My **teeth / lips** are sealed."
13. "I've just passed my driving test."
    "Oh, **felicitations / congratulations**."
14. "Things aren't going too well at work or at home."
    "Oh dear. Well, try to keep your **nose / chin** up. Things could be worse."
15. "We need your decision as soon as possible."
    "All right. Let me **sleep / dream** on it. I'll give you an answer in the morning."
16. "Can I borrow your car tonight?"
    "I'd **rather / prefer** you didn't."
17. "Can I borrow your car tonight?"
    "No way! Not a **possibility / chance**!"
18. "Would you like to come to the cinema tonight?"
    "I'd **want / love** to, thanks."
19. "Would you like to come to the cinema tonight?"
    "I can't. I'm up to my **eyeballs / nostrils** in work."
20. "I'm taking my Citizenship test tomorrow."
    "Good **chance / luck**. I'll be keeping my **legs / fingers** crossed for you."

21. "It's my birthday today."
"Oh, really? Many happy **returns / repeats**."

22. "I think the weather's going to be good this weekend."
"Yes, touch **metal / wood**."

23. "What was the name of that restaurant we went to last week?"
"It's on the tip of my **nose / tongue**. I'll remember it in a minute."

24. "Mike, could you take a photograph of us?"
"OK, pass me your camera. Right, say **cheese / chips** everyone!"

25. "I'm afraid I haven't got any coffee left. Is tea all right?"
"Sure. Any **port / harbour** in a storm."

26. "Can I borrow your mobile to make a quick call."
"Of course, by my **friend / guest**."

27. "These cakes you've made look delicious, Anne. Can I have one?"
"Yes, **serve / help** yourself."

28. "I failed my driving test again."
"Oh **bad / tough** luck!"

29. "How did you know I had an interview last week?"
"A little **insect / bird** told me."

30. "I'm off to bed. Goodnight."
"Goodnight. Sweet **sleep / dreams**."

31. (*On the phone*) "Is Alice there, please?"
"Yes, hold **up / on**, I'll just get her for you."

32. (*On the phone*) "Is Alice there, please?"
"I'm afraid she isn't. Can I take a **message / note**?"

33. "Did you enjoy the party last night?"
"Yes, it was **fun / funny**."

34. "Why did you accept the job? The pay is terrible."
"Yes, but I need some money desperately, and **beggars / scroungers** can't be choosers."

35. "I don't believe it! You've broken my favourite cup!"
"All right, keep your **hair / head** on! I'll get you another one."

36. "Did you do anything interesting over the weekend?"
"No, I just watched TV. I really must get a **life / living**."

37. (*In a restaurant, at the end of a meal*) "That was delicious. Let me pay the bill."
"No, let's go **Dutch / German** and split it."

38. "Goodbye."
"Goodbye. Take **care / caution**."

39. "I need some help cooking dinner. And the grass needs cutting. Oh, and the car needs a wash."
"Hold on! I've only got one pair of **hands / feet**!"

40. "I've got some amazing news to tell you."
"Really? Well, go on. I'm all **ears / eyes**."

Also see *Where are they?* on page 55

The UK A – Z

These exercises contain an eclectic range of words, names, places, etc, connected with the UK. Most of them do not appear anywhere else in this book.

Exercise 1: For each word or expression below, two definitions are given, (a) and (b): one is genuine, and one is nonsense. Decide which one is correct in each case.

1. *The Archers* is / are:
(a) A division of soldiers who have special responsibility for guarding the *monarch* (the King or Queen). (b) The title of a popular, long-running radio *soap opera*.

2. *Auld Lang Syne* is:
(a) A song that is traditionally sung at midnight on *New Year's Eve*. (b) The ancient right of pedestrian access across privately-owned land.

3. *Balmoral* is:
(a) The name of one of the Queen's residences in Scotland. (b) A traditional British sport, which combines elements of tennis and cricket.

4. *Ben Nevis* is:
(a) The name of the leader of the Scottish Parliament. (b) The name of the highest mountain in the UK.

5. *The Big Four* is:
(a) The collective name given to the UK's largest banks. (b) A nickname for *the Beatles*, a successful pop group from the 1960s.

6. A *chippy* is:
(a) An unemployed person. (b) An informal word for a fish and chip shop.

7. A *constable* is:
(a) A lower-ranking policeman or policewoman. (b) An administrative region in the UK (similar to a *council* or *borough*).

8. A *council house* is:
(a) A house owned by the local council, for which tenants pay a low rent. (b) The main administrative building where a council has its offices.

9. *Corrie* is:
(a) An affectionate name for British television's longest-running soap opera, *Coronation Street*. (b) An affectionate name given to anyone who comes from Wales.

10. A *cuppa* is:
(a) An informal word for a cup of tea. (b) An informal word for a policeman / woman.

11. *Crufts* is:
(a) The name of a competition for dogs that takes place every year in the UK. (b) An informal word for people who are members of the upper classes.

12. *D.I.Y.* is:
(a) A government department that promotes cooperation between young people in the UK and abroad (*The Department for International Youth*). (b) The activity of making or repairing things for your house (*do-it-yourself*).

13. *Eton* is:
(a) A cheap traditional dish made from the parts of a cow that are normally thrown away (similar to a hamburger). (b) The name of a famous *public school* near *Windsor*.

14. A *fiver* is:
(a) An informal word for a typical working week (ie, *five* days a week, from nine to *five*). (b) An informal word for a five pound (£5) note.

15. A *G and T* is:
(a) A popular alcoholic drink (a *gin and toni(c)*. (b) An informal expression for an unskilled worker (a *general and trade*).

Exercise 2: Instructions as above.

1. *God Save the Queen* is:
(a) The name of the UK's national anthem. (b) The motto of the UK.

2. A *green belt* is:
(a) An academic qualification awarded to people who complete a degree course when they are fifty or older.
(b) An area of countryside surrounding a large town or city, and which cannot be built on.

3. A *guide dog* is:
(a) The informal name given to a government adviser who helps member of the Cabinet make a decision. (b) A specially trained dog that helps blind people to become more independent.

4. The *gutter press* is:
(a) A derogatory nickname given to some of the popular newspapers that report gossip and scandal rather than news. (b) An informal name given to the national obsession for following strange diets in order to lose weight.

5. The *Home Counties* are:
(a) The counties where the Queen has one of her official residences. (b) The counties that surround London.

6. A *jumble sale* is:
(a) A transaction in which the government sells off national industries to other countries. (b) An event where people raise money by selling old things that they don't want any more.

7. A *kilt* is:
(a) An item of clothing traditionally worn by Scots. (b) A loud party involving lots of singing and dancing, usually as part of a national celebration.

8. A *lollipop lady* or *man* is:
(a) A woman or man who looks after people's children when they are at work. (b) A woman or man whose job is to help children cross the road safely (usually when they are going to or from school).

9. A *milkman* is:
(a) An informal word for a man who is not married (and usually still lives at home with his parents).
b) Someone whose job it is to deliver milk to people's houses on a regular basis.

10. *Ms* is / are:
(a) The letters that are written after the name of someone who has obtained a *Master of Sciences* degree. (b) A formal title that is used in front of a woman's surname when speaking to, or writing to, her when we don't know whether or not she is married.

11. *Nessie* is:
(a) A popular nickname for Elizabeth, the Queen of the UK. (b) A popular nickname for the *Loch Ness Monster*, a legendary monster that lives in a lake in Scotland.

12. An *offie* is:
(a) An informal word for a day off from work taken by someone who is pretending that he / she is ill. (b) An informal word for an *off licence* (a shop that sells alcohol to take away).

13. *The Old Bailey* is:
(a) A common name for the Central Criminal Court in London. (b) The name of the UK's longest-running newspaper.

14. *The Old Bill* (or sometimes just *the Bill*) is:
(a) A nickname for the police. (b) A nickname for the Bank of England.

15. *Oxbridge* is:
(a) An informal word for anyone who has been to (and graduated from) university or another form of higher education. (b) The collective name for the two famous universities of *Oxford and Cambridge*.

Exercise 3: Instructions as above.

1. *Oxfam* is:
(a) A government-backed organisation that helps British farmers get more money for their products.
(b) A charity organisation that raises money for poor people in other countries.

2. *Planning permission* is:
(a) The official permission a couple need if they want to have more than two children. (b) The permission that is needed from a local authority before carrying out certain kinds of building work.

3. A *quid* is:
(a) A very informal word for a pound (£). (b) An informal word for a child.

4. *Recess* is:
(a) The long period during the summer when Parliament stops meeting. (b) The period between one political party losing a general election, and a new political party taking over.

5. *Scotch* is:
(a) Scottish whisky. (b) A Scottish person.

6. A *senior citizen* is:
(a) Someone who is more than 60 years old. (b) Any member of the Royal Family.

7. *Speaker's Corner* is:
(a) The name of a popular political television programme. (b) A place in London where ordinary people can speak freely and publicly on any subject they like.

8. *Stilton* is:
(a) The period of the year between January 1st and Easter. (b) A strong-smelling cheese that is often eaten at Christmas.

9. A *tenner* is:
(a) An informal word for a ten pound (£10) note. (b) An informal word for a man or woman who is good at everything he / she does.

10. A *Tory* is:
(a) A slightly derogatory name for a member of the Conservative Party, or one if its supporters. (b) A town or village that has no political representation in an election.

11. *Ulster* is:
(a) Another name for the Republic of Ireland, used especially by Irish nationalists. (b) Another name for Northern Ireland, used especially by Irish unionists.

12. *V.A.T.* is:
(a) A tax on goods and services (*Value Added Tax*). (b) A famous sporting trophy for which universities compete (The *Varsity Association Trophy*)

13. A *vicar* is:
(a) A public protest against government action. (b) A priest in the Church of England.

14. *Wellies* are:
(a) People who cannot decide who to vote for in an election (from the word "*Well*..."). (b) Rubber boots (properly called *Wellingtons*) which do not let water in.

15. A *whip* is:
(a) Someone in a political party whose job is to make certain that other members go where they are needed and vote in the correct way. (b) A member of a political party who rebels against that party or one of its policies.

Utilities and services

Choose the best word or phrase to complete sentences 1 – 18. In some cases, more than one answer may be possible, and in some cases the answer depends on certain situations.

1. Water that is piped into your home is **safe / unsafe** to drink.

2. Water bills must be paid **once a year / twice a year / in ten instalments throughout the year**.

3. The amount you pay for your water depends on **the size of your property / the amount of water you use**.

4. If you receive *housing benefit* from your local *social security* office, **the cost of water bills is included in it / it does not cover the cost of water bills**.

5. Electricity is supplied to UK households at **240 / 300** volts.

6. **All / most** UK homes are supplied with gas.

7. Electricity and gas are all supplied by **the same company / different companies**.

8. *Transco* is the name of the organisation that supplies **gas / electricity** across the network to providers.

9. Most land-line telephone services in the UK are provided by **Vodafone / British Telecom**.

10. In an emergency (for example, if you need the police, an ambulance or the fire brigade), the telephone number to call is **112 / 999**.

11. Refuse (household rubbish) is collected from outside people's homes **once / twice** a week.

12. It is **possible / not possible** to leave items such as glass and paper outside your house to be collected for *recycling*.

13. You **can / cannot** leave large items such as refrigerators, televisions, etc, for refuse collection.

14. Everybody in the UK must pay a property tax which is used to pay for local government services. This is called a **council / poll** tax.

15. This tax must be paid **once a year / twice a year / in ten instalments throughout the year**.

16. If you buy a property using a mortgage, the mortgage provider will insist that you have **a full-time job / a partner (eg, a husband or wife) / household insurance**.

17. If someone lives in a council-owned property and creates excessive problems for his / her neighbours, he / she can be taken to court and **fined / evicted from his or her property.**

18. If you live in a private property and are having problems with your neighbours, the best thing to do in the first instance is **try to talk to your neighbour about it / call the police**.

Exercise 1: Look at these conversations, and complete each one with words or expressions from the box. Then decide where the speakers are in each case.

bar	cashback	change	checked in	circle	fare	half	housekeeping	luggage
matinee	meter	mini bar	packing	peak	performance	PIN	pints	platform
reception	return	room service	round	snacks	stage	yourself		

1.

Speaker 1: Here we are, mate. Town centre. That's £9.20 please.
Speaker 2: £9.20? But your (a)________ says £8.20.
Speaker 1: I know, but we charge £1 for each item of (b)________ carried.
Speaker 2: Oh, right. Well, here's £10. Keep the (c)________.
Speaker 1: Thanks mate.

2.

Speaker 1: I'd like a cheap day (a)________ to Oakford, please.
Speaker 2: It's still the (b)________ period, so I'll have to charge you full (c)________. Is that OK?
Speaker 1: I suppose so. How much will that be?
Speaker 2: £38.75. The next service goes from (d)________ 18 in five minutes.

3.

Speaker 1: Hello. Is that (a)________?
Speaker 2: Yes, sir.
Speaker 1: Good. I've just (b)________, and there don't seem to be any towels in my bathroom.
Speaker 2: Ah, you want (c)________. Call the (d)________ and they'll put you through.
Speaker 1: Thanks. Oh, while you're there, could I have some more water for the (e)________ please?

4.

Speaker 1: I'd like two tickets for this evening's (a)________, please.
Speaker 2: I'm afraid we're sold out for tonight. The only tickets we have left are for tomorrow's (b)________.
Speaker 1: Oh, I see. In that case, I'll have two for tomorrow afternoon's show.
Speaker 2: Fine. Seats in the stalls are £22, and in the (c)________ they're £18. All seats have a good view of the (d)________.

5.

Speaker 1: Good morning. Would you like any help (a)________ your bags?
Speaker 2: Hello. No, I'll manage, thanks.
Speaker 1: (*A few minutes later*) That's £56.50 please.
Speaker 2: Thanks. I'll pay for that with Maestro.
Speaker 1: Thank you. Would you like any (b)________?
Speaker 2: Not today, thanks.
Speaker 1: OK. Could you enter your (c)________ and press 'Enter', please?

6.

Speaker 1: The usual?
Speaker 2: No, it's my (a)________. Two (b)________ of lager, please. And do you do food?
Speaker 3: At lunchtime we just do (c)________. The menus are on the table. Order at the (d)________ and we'll bring your food to the table.
Speaker 2: OK. Well, I'll pay for these now.
Speaker 3: Right you are. That's £5 please.
Speaker 2: Thanks. Oh, and one for (e)________?
Speaker 3: That's very kind of you. I will, thanks. Just a (f)________.

Exercise 2: Instructions as above.

account allergy balance bill branded change deposit dessert GP hay fever pass pharmacist prescription pump receipt remedies registered reservation seat service shout statement surgery transactions unleaded withdrawal

1.

Speaker 1: Good afternoon. I'd like to order a repeat (a)________, please.
Speaker 2: Right, what's it for?
Speaker 1: It's for a salbutamol inhaler for my asthma.
Speaker 2: All right. Are you (b)________ with this (c)________?
Speaker 1: No, not yet. I've just moved to the area.
Speaker 2: Right, well, you need to fill in this form and then make an appointment to see one of our (d)________'s.

2.

Speaker 1: Hello, are you the (a)________?
Speaker 2: I am. How can I help you?
Speaker 1: Well, I've got bad (b)________. I was wondering if there are any over-the-counter (c)________ that might help.
Speaker 2: There are several, but we have our own-brand anti-(d)________ tablets, which might help. They're cheaper than any of the (e)________ products available, but they're just as good.

3.

Speaker 1: Good evening, madam. Do you have a (a)________?
Speaker 2: Yes, four for eight-thirty. The name's Ross. Helena Ross.
Speaker 1: (*2 hours later*) Was everything all right?
Speaker 2: Yes, it was very nice, thank you, but the (b)________ was a bit slow.
Speaker 1: I'm sorry about that, madam. We're a little short-staffed tonight. Would you like some (c)________?
Speaker 2: No thanks. We're running a bit late. Could we just have the (d)________ please?

4.

Speaker 1: Good afternoon. I'd like to (a)________ this cheque please. And could I check the (b)________ of my (c)________?
Speaker 2: Certainly. It currently stands at £350.
Speaker 1: That's a bit less than I thought. Could you print me out a (d)________ showing my (e)________ over the last two weeks?
Speaker 2: No problem. (A few moments later) Here you are, Mr Walton.
Speaker 1: Thanks. Mm, I don't recognise this (f)________ here. Can you find out where it was made?

5.

Speaker 1: Do you go to North Parade?
Speaker 2: I do. That's £1.60 please. Have you got the right (a)________? I'm a bit short.
Speaker 1: Actually I've got a (b)________. Could you tell me when we get there?
Speaker 2: Yes. Take a (c)________ and I'll give you a (d)________.

6.

Speaker 1: Which (a)________?
Speaker 2: Er, number 7.
Speaker 1: Number 7. 22 litres of (b)________?
Speaker 2: That's right.
Speaker 1: That's £20 exactly. Would you like a (c)________?

Exercise 3: Instructions as above. One word from the box can be used twice.

application	attendant	bags	bay	boarding pass	booked	clamped
concessions	course	delay	departure	enrol	exhibits	first class	flight
gallery	gate	guide	insurance	interfered	pack	Park and Ride
prospectus	road tax	scales	senior citizens	ticket	time limit	waiting list

1.

Speaker 1: Good morning. I'd like to send this (a)________, please.
Speaker 2: Thank you. Put it on the (b)________. That will be £1.60.
Speaker 1: Thanks. I'd also like to renew my (c)________ while I'm here.
Speaker 2: Right. I'll need your (d)________ and MOT details, please.
Speaker 1: Here you are. Oh, and have you got any passport (e)________ forms?

2.

Speaker 1: I don't believe it! I've been (a)________!
Speaker 2: Why? You bought a (b)________, didn't you?
Speaker 1: Yes, and I've only been here for four hours. You're allowed to stay in this (c)________ for up to 72 hours, so I haven't exceeded my (d)________. And I'm well inside the (e)________.
Speaker 2: Well, there's an (f)________ over there. Why don't you ask him what's happened?

3.

Speaker 1: Could you put your (a)________ on the (b)________, please? Did you (c)________ these yourself?
Speaker 2: Yes, I did.
Speaker 1: And could anyone have (d)________ with them?
Speaker 2: No, they couldn't.
Speaker 1: Thank you. Right, here's your (e)________. Seat 17F. There's a slight (f)________, I'm afraid.
Speaker 2: Oh, for how long?
Speaker 1: Not long, about 15 minutes, but watch the screens for (g)________ and (h)________ information. Have a good (i)________.

4.

Speaker 1: Do you do (a)________?
Speaker 2: We do. Children, students and (b)________ are half price. We also do a family ticket for £10.
Speaker 1: Right, well, a family ticket then, please.
Speaker 2: Here you are. That's £10 please. Would you like a (c)________? They're free.
Speaker 1: Thanks. We're particularly interested in the Egyptian section. Where's that?
Speaker 2: On this floor. Go past the gift shop and the portrait (d)________, and then turn left. They've got some wonderful (e)________. I'm sure your children will love it.

5.

Speaker 1: I'd like to (a)________ on an evening (b)________ please.
Speaker 2: Right, what are you interested in?
Speaker 1: Creative Photography for beginners.
Speaker 2: I'm afraid that one is fully (c)________ for the next 3 months. I can put you on the (d)________ if you like.
Speaker 1: Oh, well, in that case maybe I might choose something else. Do you have a (e)________ I can look at?

Also see *Spoken responses* on page 49.

A year in the UK: Traditions, holidays and other occasions 1

Complete the text with words and expressions from the box. There are some words that you do not need.

Ash Wednesday	backward	British	Burns Night	daffodil	decorations	Easter
England	English	Epiphany	forward	haggis	Ireland	Irish
leap	Lent	Mardi Gras	Mothering	Mothers'	mothers	New Year's
Pancake	resolutions	Robert Burns	Scotland	Shrove Tuesday	Saint (St) David's	Saint (St) Patrick's
Saint (St) Valentine's	Sausage	Summer	tatties and neeps	Time	twelfth night	Wales
Welsh	whisky					

January

January 1st: (**1**)__________ Day. This is a public holiday. Some people make (**2**)__________ on this day: this is a list of things that they promise to do in the coming year (for example, "I will try to be nice to people, I will give up smoking, I will go on a diet"). In (**3**)__________, January 2nd is also a public holiday.

January 6th. This day is called (**4**)__________, but most people call it (**5**)__________, and it is the last day of the Christmas period. We must remove our Christmas (**6**)__________ before the sun sets, or we will have an unlucky year.

January 25th: People in Scotland celebrate (**7**)__________, where they remember the famous Scottish poet (**8**)__________ (1759 – 1796). They celebrate by drinking (**9**)__________ and eating traditional foods such as (**10**)__________ and (**11**)__________ (potatoes and turnips).

February

(**12**)__________. This day happens 41 days before Easter (so it sometimes takes place in March). British people often call it (**13**)__________ Day, because of the food we traditionally make and eat on this day. The day after is called (**14**)__________, and is the beginning of the period called (**15**) __________: this period lasts until (**16**)__________, and some people observe it by giving up something they enjoy (such as smoking, eating chocolate, etc).

February 14th: This is (**17**)__________ Day. It is not a holiday, but is a day to tell your loved one how important they are by spending all your money on cards, presents, and an expensive meal out.

February 29th: Years in which there are 29 days in February are called (**18**)__________ years. Traditionally, this date is the only one when a woman can ask a man to marry her!

March

March 1st: (**19**)__________ Day. He is the patron saint of (**20**)__________. (**21**)__________ people often observe this day by wearing a (**22**)__________ (a spring flower that is associated with this country).

March 17th: (**23**)__________ Day. He is the patron saint of (**24**)__________ (where this day is observed as a public holiday). (**25**)__________ people all over the world celebrate this day with parties, drinking and dancing.

On the last weekend of March, we put our clocks (**26**)__________ by one hour. This is the beginning of (**27**)__________ (**28**)__________ (**29**)__________.

The Sunday three weeks before Easter is called (**30**)__________ Sunday, although most people call it (**31**)__________ Day. Children visit or send cards and flowers to their (**32**)__________.

A year in the UK: Traditions, holidays and other occasions 2

Choose the correct words and expressions in **bold** in this text.

April

April 1st. This day is called April (**1**) **Fools**' / **Twits**' Day. Traditionally, people play jokes and tricks on each other (but they are only allowed to do this until (**2**) **midday / midnight**). Newspapers and radio and television programmes often have humorous 'joke' articles or features that are designed to trick people.

(**3**) **Good / Black** Friday is an important day in the Christian calendar (it usually takes place in April, but sometimes happens in March). This commemorates the crucifixion of Jesus Christ. People in the UK observe this day by eating *hot cross* (**4**) ***cakes / buns*** (= sweet bread with fruit and spices) for (**5**) **breakfast / dinner**. Banks, post offices and many businesses are closed across the UK on this day.

Easter (**6**) **Saturday / Sunday** commemorates the resurrection of Jesus Christ, although many people in the UK treat it as a (**7**) **secular / religious** holiday. Chocolate Easter (**8**) **eggs / crosses** or chocolate rabbits and chickens are often given to children. Families often get together and eat a traditional meal of roast (**9**) **turkey / lamb**. The next day, Easter (**10**) **Sunday / Monday**, is a public holiday in England, Wales and (**11**) **Scotland / Northern Ireland**, but not in (**12**) **Scotland / Northern Ireland**.

April 21st: This is the Queen's (**13**) **birthday / Coronation day**, although it is *not* a public holiday. The Queen actually has <u>two</u> of these every year: in addition to the one in April, she has an *official* one in June!

April 23rd is St (**14**) **George's / Swithin's** Day. He is the patron saint of (**15**) **Wales / England**. People do not celebrate this day, but many churches and some public buildings fly the national flag, which is (**16**) **white with a red cross / green with a white circle**.

May

1st May (May Day) is *not* a holiday in the UK, but the first (**17**) **Monday / Friday** of the month is (so if that day falls on May 1st, then May 1st *is* a holiday). Many towns and villages hold fairs and fetes where you can see traditional events such as (**18**) **Morris / Austin** dancing, and (**19**) **maybug / maypole** dancing. The last (**20**) **Monday / Friday** of May is also a public holiday (and is called the (**21**) **Spring / Summer** Bank Holiday).

June

June 21st is the first official day of summer, and is also the (**22**) **warmest / longest** day of the year. 24th June is known as (**23**) **Whitsun / Midsummer** Day.
The third Sunday in June is (**24**) **Father's Day / Grandparents' Day**, which is similar to Mother's Day (see March on the previous page), although it is not as widely observed.

July

July 12th in Northern Ireland is a public holiday and is known as the Battle of the (**25**) **Boyne / Liffey** or *Orangemen's Day*. This was, and remains, very much a political and religious holiday with historical origins: Orangemen are (**26**) **protestants / Catholics** who want Northern Ireland to remain a part of the United Kingdom.

August

The first Monday of August is another public holiday in (**27**) **Northern Ireland / Scotland**, and the last Monday of August is a public holiday in England, Wales and Northern Ireland / Scotland.

A year in the UK: Traditions, holidays and other occasions 3

Rearrange the letters in **bold** to make words. In some cases, you will need to split these into two or more words. Write these in the appropriate space in the grid at the bottom of the page. If you do this correctly, you will reveal (in the shaded vertical section) the name of someone who plays an important role on and around December 25th. Note that you should *not* put any gaps between the words when you write them in the grid, and you should not include any apostrophes in the grid.

October 31st is called **aenloHwel** (*1 word: number 14 in the grid*), the night when all the spirits of the dead walk the earth. Children often dress as witches and ghosts, and go around people's houses saying "Trick or treat". They hope that people will give them sweets and money.

November 5th is known as **swGyFaNkheiugt** (*3 words: number 1 in the grid*). It is also known as **figbonrehtin** (*2 words: number 9 in the grid*). This commemorates the *Gunpowder Plot* (1605), in which a group of Catholics tried, and failed, to kill the protestant British king when he was visiting Parliament. We commemorate this event with fireworks and a fire.

November 11th is called **brmeyDamReance** (*2 words: number 13 in the grid*). On this day we remember the victims of wars since the beginning of the 20th century (especially the First World War, which ended at 11 o'clock on November 11th: *the 11th hour of the 11th day of the 11th month*). We commemorate this event by wearing paper *poppies* (= red flowers), and at 11 o'clock we hold a two-minute **einscle** (*1 word: number 15 in the grid*).

November 30th is **SwArae'sDtndy** (*3 words: number 2 in the grid*). He is the patron saint of **onaStldc** (*1 word: number 7 in the grid*).

At Christmas, people send cards to wish one another a "*Happy (or Merry) Christmas and a Happy New Year*". "Season's **tigensreg** (*1 word: number 3 in the grid*)" is an expression that is often written in these cards instead, especially if sent by, or to, non-Christians.

In addition to a tree and other decorations, people often hang **lyolh** (*1 word: number 4 in the grid*) and **tostilmee** (*1 word: number 11 in the grid*) in their home at Christmas.

reyukT (*1 word: number 6 in the grid*), Christmas pudding and mince pies are three foods that are often eaten on Christmas day.

December 26th is a national holiday. It is called **noDagixBy** (*2 words: number 10 in the grid*). Traditionally, it was the time when people such as the postman, the milkman, servants, etc, were given a Christmas 'box' containing money, as a reward for the work they had done. It is an important part of Christmas, and is also an important day for **tisprogn** (*1 word: number 12 in the grid*) events.

December 31st is known as **seYewNvar'Ee** (*3 words: number 5 in the grid*). In Scotland, it is called **nagHoyam** (*1 word, number 8 in the grid*).

1.
2.
3.
4.
5.
6.
7.
8.
9.
10.
11.
12.
13.
14.
15.

Answer key

Abbreviations (pages 1 – 2)

Note that in all of these abbreviations the individual letters are usually spoken (so, for example, we say *R.A.F.*, and not *Raf*). The one exception is *ASBO*, which is pronounced as one word.

Exercise 1

1. MP: *Member of Parliament*. Someone who has been elected to represent people from a particular district (called a constituency) in Parliament. In Scotland, these people are called *MSPs* (*Members of the Scottish Parliament*). The *National Assembly for Wales* and the *Northern Ireland Assembly* have *AMs* (= *Assembly Members*). **2.** BBC: *the British Broadcasting Corporation*. An organisation that broadcasts television and radio programmes and is owned by the British government. It does not have advertising and is paid for mainly by the *licence fee* (= money paid every year by people who own a television). People sometimes refer to the BBC humorously as *the Beeb*. **3.** RAF: *The Royal Air Force*. The military air force of the UK. **4.** BA: *British Airways*. The national civilian airline of the UK. **5.** PIN: *personal identification number*. A set of four numbers that you need to know when you use a credit / debit card in a shop or in a cash machine. **6.** GCSE: *General Certificate of Secondary Education*. Exams in a wide range of subjects taken by students in England and Wales, usually at the age of 15 or 16. A lot of students also take *A level exams* two years later. These are the exams that you need to take before you go to university. **7.** RSPCA: *The Royal Society for the Prevention of Cruelty to Animals*. An organisation that aims to protect and care for animals. **8.** NSPCC: *The National Society for the Prevention of Cruelty to Children*. An organisation in the UK that protects children from being treated badly. **9.** ASBO: *Antisocial Behaviour Order*. An order that can be applied for by the police against any individual over the age of 10 years old who is causing someone distress, harm or harassment. An ASBO restricts their behaviour, and can result in a fine or prison sentence if it is broken. **10.** GMT: *Greenwich Mean Time*. The time at Greenwich in England, which is used as an international standard. **11.** NHS: *The National Health Service*. A system in the UK that provides free medical care and is paid for through taxes. **12.** C of E: *The Church of England*. The official Christian Church in England that has the King or Queen as its leader. A person who goes to a *C of E* church is called an *Anglican*. In Scotland, the official church is called the *Church of Scotland*. **13.** VAT: *value added tax*. A tax that is paid on goods and services. Some goods, such as food, are *VAT-exempt*, which means that you do not pay VAT on them. **14.** AA: *The Automobile Association*. An organisation for drivers that gives its members information on travelling by road, and helps them if their car breaks own. Other similar organisations in the UK include the *RAC* (= *the Royal Automobile Club*) and *Green Flag*.

Exercise 2

1. GP: *General Practitioner*. A doctor who deals with general medical problems and treats the families in a particular area. **2.** BT: *British Telecommunications plc* (*usually just called British Telecom, or BT*). A major British telephone company. (*plc* = *public limited company*: a company in the UK that has shares that ordinary people can buy). **3.** CAB: *Citizens' Advice Bureau*. An organisation that provides a free service for people who need advice on legal, financial and other matters. **4.** NI: *National Insurance*. A system that all employers and workers pay into, providing money for people who do not have a job or are old or ill. **5.** TUC: *the Trades Union Congress*. The organisation that represents British trade unions. **6.** ID: *Identification*. At the time this book was being written, it was not a legal requirement for people to carry ID at all times. **7.** MOT: *Ministry of Transport*. An official test that all cars over three years old must have each year to check that they are safe to drive. **8.** DVLA: *the Driver and Vehicle Licensing Agency*. The government organisation that is responsible for providing people with driving licences and collecting road tax. **9.** PG: *parental guidance*. A code used for describing a film (at the cinema, or on a video or DVD) that contains scenes, subjects or language that might be considered unsuitable for children who are younger than 13. The other film codes used in Britain are: *U* (= *universal*; suitable for anyone aged four or over); *12* (= should only be watched by people who are at least 12 years old, unless they have someone over 18 with them); *15* (= should only be watched by people who are at least 15 years old); *18* (= should only be watched by people who are at least 18 years old). **10.** FE: *Further Education*. Courses of study or training that some people do after they have left school, especially if they do not go to university. An FE college is sometimes called a *CFE* (*College of Further Education*). **11.** ESOL: *English for Speakers of Other Languages*. The activity of teaching and learning English to / for people whose first language is not English. **12.** FCO: *Foreign and Commonwealth Office*. The official name for the British Foreign Office (= the government department that deals with Britain's relations with foreign countries). **13.** A and E (also *A & E*): *Accident and Emergency*. A department in a hospital that deals with emergencies. **14.** BA: *Bachelor of Arts*. A first degree in a subject such as languages or history from a university. A first degree in a scientific subject is a *BSc* (= *Bachelor of Science*). An advanced degree is called an *MA* or an *MSc* (= *Master of Arts / Master of Science*).

Exercise 3

We have an attractive furnished and **self-contained** one-**bedroom** flat to rent **near** the town of Woodstock. The flat benefits from **central heating** and has all the **modern conveniences** that you would expect in a property of this class. We would prefer you to be a **non-smoker**. We will not allow pets in our property. The rent is £700 **per calendar month**, which includes bills. You will also need to pay a **deposit** when you move in. You will need to rent the flat for a **minimum** of six **months**.

I am selling my metallic black 2002 model Mazda MX5 1.8. It is in **excellent** condition. It has **air-conditioning** to keep you cool in summer, and **power steering** which makes it easy to turn the car around. It has been serviced

Answer key

recently, and it has a **full service history** so that you know it has been well-maintained. The MOT is valid until the **end of** the year. I am selling it for £9500, **or nearest offer**.

Cultural do's and don'ts (page 3)

1. ...*when they have invited you for drinks, dinner etc* = unacceptable. It is polite to take a small gift, such as a bottle of wine, chocolates or flowers. **2.** ...*their politics* = unacceptable. **3.** ...*they earn* = unacceptable. **4.** ...*they are* = unacceptable, unless this information is needed for something. **5.** ...*to show your appreciation for the food* = unacceptable. **6.** ...*in front of other people* = acceptable. **7.** ...*on their clothes or possessions* = acceptable (and the person being complimented should thank you for your compliments). **8.** ...*to other road users* = unacceptable. Bad manners on the road, including failing to indicate when turning, driving too close behind someone, or suddenly driving in front of another driver so he has to slow down quickly, can result in something called 'road rage', where the other driver becomes very angry. **9.** ...*on the ground* = unacceptable. You can be fined by the police for dropping litter. **10.** ...*walking along the street* = acceptable. **11.** ...*fingers* = acceptable, but it depends where you are and what you are eating. At a party, for example, you might be offered 'finger food' such as sandwiches, nuts, etc, which you eat with your fingers. **12.** ..."*Please*" *or* "*Thank you*" = unacceptable. Together with "Sorry" and "Excuse me", these are probably the most important English words, and we use them all the time! **13.** ...*shaking hands or kissing them* = acceptable. British people usually only shake hands in formal situations and when meeting someone for the first time. Kissing when greeting (and saying goodbye) is usually only done between family members and close friends. **14.** ...*your boyfriend, girlfriend, husband, wife, etc, in public places* = acceptable. **15.** ...*are talking to you* = acceptable, if it is done politely. **16.** ... *thanking your host for his / her hospitality* = unacceptable. **17.** ...*about someone's skin colour, religion, culture, sexuality, etc* = (very) unacceptable. **18.** ...*a meal in a restaurant* = acceptable (when we eat in a restaurant, the bill is normally divided equally among the people who have eaten, regardless of who had what to eat, drink, etc). **19.** ...*when you are in the pub with friends* = unacceptable. We take it in turns to buy drinks for the people we are with. This is called 'buying a round'. **20.** ...*in front of the person who has bought it for you* = acceptable (and you should show suitable appreciation, even if you do not like the present!). **21.** ...*at people* = unacceptable. Staring at someone can sometimes be seen as aggressive behaviour, and could get you into trouble. **22.** ...*with someone during a discussion* = acceptable, if it is done politely. **23.** ...*at a bus stop, in a shop, etc* = (very) unacceptable. British people get very angry with anyone who 'jumps the queue'. **24.** ...*that is given to you, at a dinner party for example* = (usually) acceptable if you have a good reason (for example, your religion, your principles or an allergy may prevent you from eating certain foods). **25.** ...*you do not hear or understand them* = unacceptable. It is more polite to say "Sorry?" or "Excuse me?". **26.** ...*without asking them for their permission first* = unacceptable. **27.** ...*when you are buying something in a shop* = unacceptable, but it depends where you are: some smaller shops might be prepared to give you a discount in certain situations, for example, if the thing you are buying is slightly damaged or has been used as a display item, or even if a local competitor is offering a lower price. **28.** ...*speaking with people you don't know very well* = acceptable (for example, it's cold, windy and raining very heavily. You go into a shop and the assistant says to you "Lovely weather, isn't it?"). **29.** ...*in a pub or restaurant if you are 'caught short' in the street* = (usually) acceptable, if you ask the owner first. If you go into a pub, it might be considered prudent and polite to buy a drink afterwards. **30.** ...*with your shoes on* = (generally) unacceptable, but many British people do wear their outside shoes in the house. **31.** ...*to get someone's attention in a pub, restaurant, shop, etc* = unacceptable. You should try to make eye contact with the person you want, or raise your hand slightly to get their attention. **32.** ...*invited to an informal party* = acceptable. The British are usually very punctual, but this is the one exception where it is considered rude to arrive on time or early!

Education (pages 4 – 5)

Exercise 1:

1. nursery **2.** state **3.** co-educational **4.** primary **5.** secondary **6.** uniform **7.** voluntary **8.** public **9.** home-school **10.** religious **11.** careers **12.** further **13.** higher **14.** GCSE (= *General Certificate of Secondary Education*) **15.** Languages **16.** A-Levels (*A = Advanced*) **17.** prosecuted **18.** compulsory **19.** National Curriculum

Exercise 2:

1. gap **2.** enrolment (from the verb *to enrol*) **3.** undergraduate* **4.** fees **5.** loan **6.** grant **7.** Bachelor of Arts **8.** lecture **9.** seminar (note that a teacher at university is usually called a *lecturer*. When a university teacher helps individual students or small groups of students with their studies, he / she is called a *tutor*) **10.** tutorial **11.** postgraduate (this can also be an adjective: *postgraduate studies*) **12.** continuous

*Note that a graduate is someone who has successfully finished a first degree course at university. *Graduate* can also be a verb (*He graduated from Leeds University with a degree in Biology*).

Employment 1: Job applications (pages 6 – 7)

Part 1:

1. vacancy **2.** hire or recruit **3.** staff **4.** advertises **5.** post or position **6.** internally **7.** externally **8.** agency **9.** work (*job* is countable, and should be preceded by an article or pronoun) **10.** description **11.** applicant **12.** applying **13.** requirements **14.** qualifications **15.** experience **16.** qualities **17.** practical **18.** professional **19.** rewards *or* remuneration

Answer key

20. salary (a *wage* is paid daily or weekly) **21.** rises or increments (with a slight difference in meaning: a pay *rise* might be the result of promotion or hard work, an *increment* is usually automatic and based on the length of time with the company). **22.** benefits **23.** leave *or* holidays **24.** package (we often use the expression *a rewards and benefits package*) **25.** commensurate **26.** discriminate **27.** disability

Part 2:
1. curriculum vitae (usually shortened to *CV*) *or* résumé **2.** covering **3.** suitable **4.** fill in or fill out **5.** application **6.** submit *or* send **7.** short-list **8.** interview **9.** reject *or* turn down **10.** unsuitable **11.** candidates *or* applicants **12.** potential **13.** appearance **14.** disposition **15.** skills *or* abilities **16.** literate **17.** interests *or* hobbies **18.** background **19.** medical **20.** criminal **21.** identification **22.** permit **23.** matches **24.** profile *or* criteria **25.** offered **26.** references (*referees* in this context are the people who write the references) **27.** employer **28.** colleague *or* co-worker **29.** induction **30.** temporary **31.** trial *or* probationary **32.** permanent **33.** training **34.** appraisal

Employment 2: Earnings, rewards and benefits (pages 8 – 9)

1. salary **2.** remuneration **3.** overtime **4.** increment **5.** Tax / Revenue / Customs **6.** return **7.** National Insurance **8.** deduction **9.** minimum wage **10.** double time **11.** pension plan **12.** rise (or a *raise*) **13.** advance **14.** payslip **15.** bonus **16.** payroll **17.** package **18.** weighting (for example, a job advertisement might offer an annual salary of £32000 + £5000 London *weighting*) **19.** leave entitlement* **20.** Income / expenditure **21.** satisfaction **22.** commission **23.** incentive plans **24.** rate **25.** redundancy pay **26.** discount **27.** relocation allowance **28.** profit sharing **29.** gross **30.** net **31.** index-linked **32.** performance-related **33.** commensurate **34.** maternity / paternity **35.** unemployment benefit

* By law, everyone who is in full-time employment and who is 16 or over is entitled to at least 4 weeks of paid leave each year.

Employment 3: Workplace issues (page 10)

1. trade union **2.** retirement **3.** health and safety **4.** verbal (= spoken) warning **5.** discrimination **6.** supervisor **7.** redundancy pay **8.** notice **9.** absenteeism **10.** self-employed **11.** maternity leave **12.** harassment **13.** misconduct **14.** exploitation **15.** allowance

The expression in the shaded vertical strip (which can also be used to complete sentence 16) is *unfair dismissal*.

UK facts and figures (pages 11 – 12)

1. *Partly* true. The UK is a union of four countries: England, Scotland, Wales and Northern Ireland (*Ireland* – also called Eire – is a republic, and has been separate from the UK since 1921). **2.** The United Kingdom of Great Britain and Northern Ireland. **3.** False. Great Britain (usually shortened to *Britain*) comprises England, Scotland and Wales only. **4.** No. The main UK Parliament is based in London, but Scotland, Wales and Northern Ireland have some independent political control (through the Scottish Parliament, the Assembly for Wales and the Northern Ireland Assembly) and to some degree are able to make their own laws. Some other areas, such as the Channel Islands and the Isle of Man, also have greater or lesser degrees of autonomy. **5.** The monarch (currently Queen Elizabeth II). **6.** Welsh in Wales (where it is taught in all schools); Gaelic in Scotland. **7.** Yes, they are Scottish, Welsh and Irish (with *British / UK* citizenship). **8.** Edinburgh, Cardiff, Belfast. **9.** (d) about 59 million (58.8 to be more precise: England = 49.1 million; Scotland = 5.1 million; Wales = 2.9 million; Northern Ireland = 1.7 million). Note: a census is carried out every 10 years. The next one will be in 2011. **10.** True. **11.** White: 92%; Mixed: 1.2%; Asian or Asian British: 4%; Black or Black British: 2%; Chinese: 0.4%; Other: 0.4%. **12.** People of Indian descent. **13.** London (where they make up 29% of the capital's residents). Other areas where there are concentrations of ethnic minorities are the West Midlands, the South East, the North West and Yorkshire / Humberside. **14.** (c) 75%. **15.** Buddhism, Sikhism, Hinduism, Islam, Christianity, Judaism. (People who follow these faiths are called: *Buddhists*, *Sikhs*, *Hindus*, *Muslims*, *Christians*, *Jews*). **16.** About 70% (3% of people with a religion say that they are Muslim, and 1% say that they are Hindu). **17.** Between 8% and 11% in England and Wales. More people attend church in Scotland and Northern Ireland. **18.** (d) 1534. **19.** The Supreme Governor is the head of the Church of England. The monarch has this role, so the current Supreme Governor is Queen Elizabeth II. The most senior bishop, and the person who effectively 'runs' the Church of England, is the *Archbishop of Canterbury*. In theory he is appointed by the monarch, but in practice is appointed by the Prime Minister following the recommendations of a committee which is appointed by the church. **20.** Catholic (also called *Roman Catholic*, of which about 10% of UK worshippers are followers). The others are denominations of the *Protestant* church. (The Anglican Church is also known as the *Church of England*, often called the *C of E*. Baptists and Methodists are the two most widespread denominations in Wales, Presbyterians are members of the established church – the *Kirk* – in Scotland). **21.** About 600 miles (about 1000km). **22.** About 320 miles (about 500km). **23.** (a) Newcastle-upon-Tyne; (b) Birmingham; (c) Liverpool; (d) London; (e) Glasgow. **24.** London, Birmingham, Leeds, Glasgow, Sheffield, Bradford, Edinburgh, Liverpool, Manchester, Bristol, Cardiff, Coventry, Leicester, Belfast, Nottingham. Note that the cities listed here are in order of size (of the 15 cities listed here, London has the biggest population, Nottingham has the smallest). **25.** 18 (for men and women. This age was lowered from 21 in 1969. Women

Answer key

over 30 gained the right to vote and stand for Parliament in 1918. In 1928 they were allowed to do so from the age of 21). **26.** The Red Lion, the Rose and Crown, and the White Hart are not political parties (however, they are common names of *pubs*). **27.** Services, and especially banking, insurance and business services. Primary energy production accounts for about 10% of GDP. Electronics, chemicals and tourism are other important contributors to the UK economy. **28.** (a) approximately 5% (in 2006). **29.** No. **30.** Yes, but they are excluded from ground combat positions, and also from some naval postings. **31.** (f) 75%. **32.** No in both cases. **33.** No, they are all *illegal substances*. **34.** No. Capital punishment for murder was abolished in 1965. Corporal punishment was abolished in stages in Britain between 1948 and 1998, and in Northern Ireland in 1969. **35.** (a) 1 in 3. **36.** (a) 16, (b) 18, (c) 17, (d) 16, (e) 18, (f) 16, (g) 16 (this is called the *age of consent*).

Food (pages 13 – 14)

Exercise 1:

1. D **2.** K **3.** P **4.** Q **5.** W **6.** M **7.** V **8.** H **9.** O **10.** B **11.** E **12.** Y **13.** I **14.** J **15.** G **16.** S **17.** U **18.** R (if you use beef instead of lamb, it is a *cottage pie*) **19.** T **20.** C **21.** F **22.** Z (ironically, despite its Indian origins, the chicken version of this dish was recently voted the most "British" dish in the UK!) **23.** A **24.** L **25.** X (also called *Welsh rarebit*) **26.** N

Exercise 2:

The following foods do not belong (their country or region of origin is shown in brackets)
1. couscous (North Africa) **2.** tagine (North Africa) **3.** goulash (Hungary) **4.** jerk chicken (Jamaica) **5.** saganaki (Greece) **6.** bratwurst (Germany) **7.** caviar (Russia / Iran) **8.** kimchi (Korea) **9.** blini (Russia) **10.** piri-piri chicken (Portugal / Africa)

Healthcare (pages 15 – 16)

Exercise 1:

1. NHS (= *National Health Service*) **2.** GP (= *General Practitioner*) **3.** surgery **4.** treatment **5.** mental **6.** cure / specialist **7.** register* **8.** medical card **9.** health authority **10.** prescription **11.** dispensary (a dispensary is usually called a chemist, pharmacy or dispensing chemist) **12.** A and E (= Accident and Emergency: these are not available in all hospitals) **13.** ambulance **14.** 999 / 112 **15.** paramedics **16.** patient **17.** health check **18.** NHS Direct**

* Note that in the UK, male and female doctors treat both male and female patients. If it is important that if you want to see either a male or a female doctor, you should check that your local health care centre can / will allow this before you register. You should also check that the centre can provide specific health care services that you might need (for example, if you need maternity services, if you need a paediatrician for your child, etc).

** You can also contact this organisation on the Internet at *www.nhsdirect.nhs.uk*

Exercise 2:

1. appointment **2.** interpreter **3.** symptoms **4.** diagnosis **5.** house calls **6.** confidence **7.** vaccinations **8.** income support (= money people receive from the government if they are out of work or earning a very low wage)* **9.** out-patients (an *out-patient*, sometimes also called a *day patient*, is someone who goes to hospital and comes out on the same day. Patients who stay in a hospital overnight are called *in-patients*) **10.** Visiting hours **11.** dentist** **12.** optician **13.** midwives **14.** complications

* Note that prescriptions are free for anyone under 25 in Wales. Prescriptions are also free for anyone who has had a baby in the past 12 months, who is aged 60 or over, who is suffering from a specified medical condition or who is receiving other financial benefits such as an income-based Jobseeker's Allowance or Disabilities Tax Credit.

** Dental treatment is free for anyone under 18, pregnant women (and those who have had a baby in the last 12 months), and people on certain types of benefit. In Wales, it is free to anyone under 25 or over 60. For most other people, a charge is made.

Help and information (pages 17 – 18)

Exercise 1:

1. directory **2.** Yellow Pages / organisations **3.** Thomson Local / maps / clubs **4.** National newspapers / sporting **5.** Local newspapers / property / vehicles / events or entertainment **6.** tourist information centre **7.** Teletext / Ceefax **8.** stations / entertainment / DAB or digital (= *Digital Audio Broadcasting*) **9.** terrestrial / digital / freeview / subscription / cable / satellite / licence **10.** Citizens' Advice **11.** Libraries / borrowing / DVDs / computer / reference / Membership **12.** lost / directions / police officer / police station **13.** post office / parcels / cash / bills / tax / passport / National Savings and Investments / government **14.** Internet / Internet café / search engine / Google / Yahoo / website

Exercise 2:

1. Refugee Council (He could also call *the Immigration Advisory Service* on 020 7378 9191) **2.** HM Revenue and Customs **3.** DVLA **4.** BT Customer Services **5.** Crimestoppers **6.** Equal Opportunities Commission **7.** Seniorline **8.** Shelterline **9.** Samaritans **10.** Parentline Plus **11.** Transco **12.** NHS Direct **13.** Childline **14.** Victim Supportline

Telephone directories have a comprehensive list of telephone helplines (together with websites and addresses). These can be found at the front of the directory.

- Note that when we say telephone numbers, we usually speak each number individually. For example: *020*

Answer key

7837 7324 is usually spoken as '*Oh two oh / seven eight three seven / seven three two four*'.

- If a number is doubled, we normally say '*double*' before it. For example: *0845 601 5884* is usually spoken as '*Oh eight four five / six oh one / five double eight four*'.
- If a telephone number has one or more zeros after a number, and no numbers after it, we often say it as one number. For example: *0800 800 151* is often spoken as '*Oh eight hundred / eight hundred / one five one*'.
- Six-figure numbers are becoming increasingly spoken as three separate numbers. For example: *0800 201215* is spoken as '*Oh eight hundred / twenty / twelve / fifteen*'.

History 1 (page 19)

Here are the complete sentences

Julius Caesar led the Roman army on an exploratory foray into Britain in 55BC.

The Emperor Claudius led the Romans on a successful invasion of Britain, resulting in a period of Roman rule lasting for almost 400 years.

Queen Boudicca, a Briton of the Iceni tribe, led an unsuccessful rebellion against the Roman occupation.

The Emperor Hadrian built a wall (which can still be seen) in the north of the country to protect Britain from the Celts in (what is now) Scotland.

Jutes, Angles and Saxons from Denmark and North Germany began invading the country.

Missionaries from Rome, and monks from Ireland, began to spread Christianity across Britain.

Vikings from Denmark and Norway invaded, and many then settled and farmed.

King Alfred (known as Alfred the Great) of the Kingdom of Wessex united the Saxons and defeated the Danish and Viking armies.

William, the Duke of Normandy in France, led the last successful invasion of Britain and defeated the Saxon King Harold at the Battle of Hastings in 1066.

The Domesday Book (the first ever census of property values) was compiled and written.

The first charter of rights, called *Magna Carta*, was signed by King John after he was forced to do so by the great barons. This effectively showed that the power of the King was not absolute.

King Edward II was defeated by the Scot Robert the Bruce at the Battle of Bannockburn in 1314.

Geoffrey Chaucer wrote his literary masterpiece, *The Canterbury Tales*.

William Caxton started using Britain's first printing press (introduced from Germany).

King Henry VII won the Battle of Bosworth, which ended the Wars of the Roses and established the Tudor dynasty. The Tudors ruled England for 118 years and introduced some of the most profound changes to the country.

King Henry VIII broke from the Church of Rome and, in a period known as *the Reformation*, established the Church of England.

The laws of England began to be imposed on Wales in 1536.

Elizabeth, Henry's daughter by one of his marriages, became Queen when her half-sister Queen Mary died childless. During her reign, art and literature flourished.

The Spanish Armada, a fleet of ships sent to conquer England and restore the Catholic faith in 1588, was defeated.

William Shakespeare wrote some of the most famous literary works in the world, including *Romeo and Juliet, Hamlet and The Merchant of Venice*.

History 2 (page 20)

1. James VI / James I **2.** English Civil War **3.** republic / Oliver Cromwell **4.** monarchy / Charles II **5.** William of Orange **6.** Battle of the Boyne / Ireland **7.** Scotland / Act of Union **8.** House of Windsor / George I **9.** Bonnie Prince Charlie / Battle of Culloden **10.** Industrial Revolution **11.** War of Independence / India **12.** Napoleon Bonaparte / Battle of Waterloo **13.** Emancipation Act / slavery **14.** First World war **15.** Suffragette Movement / vote **16.** Irish / Ireland / Republic of Ireland **17.** Winston Churchill

History 3 (page 21)

1. Labour **2.** the National Health Service (the NHS) **3.** the railways **4.** 1953 **5.** India **6.** the Commonwealth **7.** "Iron Curtain" (an expression coined by Winston Churchill) **8.** Bangladesh **9.** Harold Wilson **10.** strikes **11.** the EEC (the European Economic Community, now called the EU – the European Union) **12.** Margaret Thatcher **13.** Conservative **14.** privatised **15.** 1997 **16.** remained under private ownership **17.** devolution **18.** Good Friday **19.** 2001 and 2005 **20.** better off than (although there is now a bigger gap between the rich and the poor, and about 17% of the population still live below the 'poverty line').

Housing and accommodation (pages 22 – 23)

Here is the complete text:

About 66% of the UK population own or are buying their own home. The rest live in accommodation that they **rent**.

Most people buy their property using a **mortgage** (a special kind of loan specifically for buying property, available from banks or **building societies**). On average, these are paid back over 25 years. It is important that you are able to pay this money regularly, otherwise you risk losing your property to the lender.

Most property in the UK is sold through an **estate agency** which can be found on most high streets. If a property is for sale and you are interested in buying it, you will need to make an **appointment** to **view** it. If the price of a property is too high for you, it is considered acceptable to make a lower **offer** to the seller. When you indicate that you want to buy a property, it is important that your offer is 'subject to **contract**', which means that you can **withdraw** from the sale for any reason before any papers

Answer key

are signed.

When buying a property, you should always employ the services of a good **surveyor** to carry out a thorough **survey** (to make sure that the property is in good condition, and that no **repairs** need to be made). It is also essential that you employ the services of a good **solicitor**, who will carry out various legal **checks** on the property.

Accommodation can be rented from a local **authority** (such as your local council). You will need to get your name on a **waiting** list known as a housing **register**. This housing is allocated on a **priority** basis: people with the greatest needs are **allocated** housing before anyone else (for example, people with young children, women who are expecting a baby, etc).

Accommodation can also be rented from housing **associations**. These are **independent** organisations that provide accommodation for people who need it. They do not make a **profit**. Many offer shared-**ownership** schemes for people who want to own property but who cannot afford it.

A lot of property is privately owned and rented out by **landlords**. They often run their property through a **letting** agency, but many advertise their property themselves in newspapers. If you rent accommodation this way, you will be expected to sign a contract known as a **lease** (also called a **tenancy** agreement). In most cases, you will be expected to pay a **deposit** (usually one month's rent, which you should get back when you leave the property, provided the property and everything in it is in good condition). Rent is then normally paid monthly in **advance**, which means that you pay for each month you are there at the beginning of that month.

Before you agree to move into rented accommodation, you should always check a few important points: whether the accommodation is **furnished** (are there beds, sofas, etc already in the property?), how long the **tenancy** lasts (most are for six months, with an option to extend at the end of that period), and whether or not there are any special rules (for example, many landlords specify that you cannot smoke in their property, or that you cannot have pets). If you break these rules, you could be **evicted** (told to leave the property).

Note that the person living in rented accommodation (the **tenant**) cannot be forced out of their home without being given sufficient **notice** (a written note that they must leave the property). Also note that landlords cannot **discriminate** against someone because of their sex, race, religion, etc (in other words, it is illegal to refuse someone accommodation on these grounds).

People who are unemployed or on a low income could be entitled to receive housing **benefit**. This is money which is paid by the local authority to cover all or part of the rent.

Legal matters 1 (page 24)

1. (b) The Home Secretary (although individual police forces decide what sort of work they should do in a particular area). **2.** forces. **3.** Usually no. Some specially-trained officers carry guns (also called *firearms*) in certain situations and in certain places (for example, areas where there is a high risk of terrorist activity, such as at airports or outside major government buildings). **4.** 999 or 112 (but only in emergencies). This number can also be called if you need an ambulance, the fire service, mountain rescue, cave rescue or the coastguard. **5.** Yes, certain types of crime can be reported online (through the police website *www.online.police.uk*). **6.** Yes to both. Penalties for carrying a (potentially) lethal weapon can result in a prison sentence. **7.** Life / property / disturbances (they must *keep the peace*) / crime. **8.** Yes, you can. Misconduct (= rudeness, abuse, racial or sexual discrimination, etc) is taken very seriously. You can complain in person or by writing to your local police station. Alternatively, you can write to the Chief Constable of the force involved, or contact the Independent Police Complaints Commission. **9.** They can stop you if you are on foot and search you if they think that a crime has, or might / is going to, take place, or if they think you are carrying a weapon, drugs, etc. They can stop you in a vehicle at any time and search it. **10.** You should give them your name and address, but you do not have to give them any other information (although most people do if asked). **11.** You can ask them for their name, the police station they work from, and the reason why they have stopped you. **12.** If you use abusive language or threats of violence, you could be arrested. **13.** warrant / magistrate / arrest / save / damage / disturbance. **14.** caution / evidence / interpreter / solicitor / duty / solicitor / message / practice. **15.** Yes, if you are victim of violent crime. The Criminal Injuries Compensation Authority is an organisation that pays compensation to victims of violent crime, provided the crime is reported immediately to the police, and the application for compensation is made within two years of the crime taking place.

Legal matters 2 (pages 25 – 26)

Exercise 1:

1. small claims court **2.** Court of Appeal (also called an *Appeal Court*) **3.** lawyer **4.** witness **5.** County Court (there are about 270 County Courts in England and Wales. They are presided over by either district judges or circuit judges. They deal mainly with claims regarding money, but also deal with family matters, bankruptcies and claims concerning land) **6.** European Court of Human Rights **7.** employment tribunal **8.** Magistrates' Court **9.** magistrate **10.** Citizens' Advice (sometimes abbreviated to *CAB*) **11.** Crown Court **12.** jury (a person who serves on a jury is called a *juror*) **13.** Jury service **14.** rent tribunal **15.** High Court **16.** European Court of Justice (*ECJ* for short. It is also called the *Court of Justice of the European Communities*) **17.** solicitor **18.** No win, no fee **19.** barrister **20.** House of Lords **21.** coroner's court (an investigation held here is called an *inquest*) **22.** coroner **23.** judge **24.** CPS (= Crown Prosecution Service) **25.** youth court **26.** suspect **27.** sentence **28.** defendant **29.** Legal aid **30.** dispute

Note that there are several differences between the court systems in Scotland and Northern Ireland (for example, there are 15 people on a jury in Scotland, and cases are heard in a Sheriff's Court). For more information on these systems, go to the following websites:

- www.scotcourts.gov.uk
- www.courtsni.gov.uk

Exercise 2:
1. solicitor(s) / County Court **2.** Citizens' Advice / employment tribunal **3.** small claims court **4.** rent tribunal **5.** dispute / High Court / Court of Appeal **6.** Magistrates' Court / magistrate / Crown Court / barrister (or lawyer) / jury / judge / sentences

Leisure (pages 27 – 28)

Across:
5. Wimbledon **6.** holiday **7.** National Trust **10.** library **11.** exhibitions **15.** freeview **18.** Prevention / Cruelty **23.** footpaths **24.** Grand National **25.** damage **26.** museums / galleries

Down:
1. cricket **2.** bank **3.** alcohol **4.** licence **8.** activities **9.** Ordnance Survey **12.** public house **13.** Adult education **14.** bed / breakfast **16.** parental guidance **17.** concessions **19.** Cup Final **20.** lottery **21.** commercials **22.** gambling

The monarchy (page 29)

1. Britain has a **constitutional monarchy**, which means that the powers and rights of the King or Queen (the monarch) are limited by the basic laws and principles of the country. **2.** The name of the current monarch is Queen **Elizabeth** II, and she has **reigned** the country since 1952. **3.** Her official London residence is at **Buckingham Palace**, but she has other residences around the country that she uses. **4.** Her husband is called Prince **Phillip** (the **Duke** of **Edinburgh**) and they have four children. **5.** Their eldest child is **Charles** (the **Prince** of **Wales**, and the person who will eventually succeed the Queen: he is the **heir** to the **throne**). **6.** Her other children are Prince **Andrew** (the Duke of York), Prince **Edward** (the Earl of Wessex) and Princess **Anne** (known as the *Princess Royal*). **7.** Collectively, they are known as the **Royal Family**, and are sometimes referred to as the House of Windsor (after their family name, which changed from *Saxe-Coburg* during the First World War). **8.** The monarch is the Head of State of the United Kingdom, and is also the monarch or head of state of many of the countries in the British **Commonwealth** (an organisation of countries that used to be under the political control of the UK). She is also the head of the **Church** of **England**. **9.** The monarch's limited powers and rights (see number 1 above) are known as the royal **prerogative**. However, her role is one of a **figurehead** (a leader with no real power of influence) and is largely **ceremonial**. **10.** For example, she meets and greets foreign heads of state. Each year she also opens **Parliament** and gives the **Queen's speech**, in which she outlines the **policies** of the government for the coming year. **11.** This speech does not express her views: it expresses the views of the **Prime Minister** and the **ruling** political party. **12.** The monarch must accept any decisions made by the **Cabinet** and by Parliament. **13.** The monarch cannot voice **support** for or **opposition** to the government. However, he or she can **advise**, **warn** and **encourage** the government, usually at a weekly meeting with the Prime Minister. **14.** Following advice from the Prime Minister, the monarch can **appoint** people to high positions in the **government**, the **Church** of **England** and the **armed forces**. **15.** The monarchy is very popular in Britain, although increasing numbers of people want to remove the current system and replace it with a **republic** and an elected **President**.

Money and finance (pages 30 – 31)

1. The pound sterling (shown by the symbol £. There are 100 *pence* in the pound). **2.** (a) £5, (b) £10, (c) £20, (d) £50 (*Coins* come in denominations of 1p, 2p, 5p, 10p, 20p, 50p, £1 and £2). **3.** Yes. And banknotes printed by the *Bank of England* are legal tender in Scotland and Northern Ireland. **4.** No, the United Kingdom does not use the Euro. Some larger shops in popular tourist areas may accept Euros, although they will give customers change in sterling. They may also accept US dollars. **5.** If you are changing foreign currency in a bank or foreign exchange (also called a *bureau de change*). The *exchange rate* is the value of the money of one country when you change it into the money of another country. *Commission charges* refer to the money you must pay for the bank, etc, to change your money. **6.** Some form of *identification* that shows your name and the place where you live (for example, a *utilities bill*, a passport, a driving licence, etc). **7.** Among other things, banks can sell you insurance, exchange foreign currency, arrange and act as executors for *wills*, offer financial advice, and offer special banking services for small companies and independent *traders*. You can also invest money in shares through a bank, send money abroad and pay household bills. **8.** A *loan* is money that you borrow in order to buy something. A *mortgage* is a special kind of loan used to buy a house or other building over a period of time. **9.** Banks and building societies provide almost identical financial services. However, building societies are generally considered to be better places to save money (they pay higher *interest*), and also to get a mortgage if you want to buy a house (because they charge a lower rate of *interest*). **10.** The main reason is that many UK companies pay their employees' salaries directly into their bank account. **11.** (d) a (bank) statement. A *balance* is the amount of money you have in your account. **12.** An overdraft facility lets you take money from your account even when there is no money in it. There is a limit to the amount you can take out, and in most cases you will need to pay

Answer key

interest when this happens. **13.** A credit card (for example, *Visa, American Express*) allows you to buy something from a shop and pay for it later. A debit card (for example, *Maestro*) is a substitute for cash: money is taken directly from your bank account. **14.** You can use a debit card to pay for products and services in shops, etc. A cash card can only be used to withdraw money from a *cash machine* (often called a *Cashpoint*, although this is a registered trade name for the cash machines used by Lloyds TSB). Most debit cards have a cash withdrawal facility, but not all cash cards have a payment facility. **15.** *Personal identification number*. You will need to enter this into a cash machine before you withdraw cash, and you will need to enter it into a hand-held computer when you use a card in a shop. **16.** Sometimes. It depends on the company that owns and operates the machine. **17.** The shop can give you some cash from the till, and the total amount of cash you take will be added to your shopping bill. Many people use this system in addition to using a cash machine, to withdraw cash. **18.** A store card works like a credit card, but you can only use it in that store or chain. Store cards have received a lot of criticism because many of them charge a very high rate of interest. **19.** They offer customers a *high credit limit*, but they also charge high *rates of interest*, especially if the customer fails to pay off his / her *balance*, or part of that balance, within a specified time. **20.** APR = *Annual Percentage Rate*, the rate of interest that you must pay over a year when you borrow money (for example, if you borrow £1000 at an APR of 10%, and you pay the money back over 1 year, you will need to pay a total of £1100). **21.** (a) an ISA (*Individual Savings Account*). People who hold an ISA can put in a limited amount of money each year (currently up to £3000), and interest is calculated and paid at the end of the *financial year* (at the beginning of April). A lot of different banks, building societies and finance companies offer ISAs, with varying rates of interest. **22.** This is an order to your bank to regularly pay money from your account to a person or organisation. **23.** Both systems work in similar ways. However, with *direct debit*, the amount of money that goes out of your account can change, and this amount is decided by the person or company you are paying (for example, an electric bill, which changes each *quarter*). With a standing order, the amount of money stays the same each time. **24.** If you are refused credit, a bank or other company refuses to let you borrow money, often because you have a bad *credit rating*. You can ask the company why they are refusing to lend you money, and you can check your credit rating (for a fee) with a *credit reference agency*. **25.** (a), (d), (g), (i) and (j) are supermarkets or department stores. **26.** This is an informal expression which means that you have less than £0 in your account. In other words, you are *overdrawn*. If you have money in your account, we can say that you are *in the black*. **27.** The post office. *National Savings and Investments* is a government-backed savings and investments service that operates through the post office. **28.** *Online* shopping / banking is done on the *Internet*. The 🔒 symbol shows you that you are using a secure site, and no one can access the information you are entering on your computer. **29.** (b) (insurance) brokers. Many people buy insurance directly from the insurance companies themselves, as this is often cheaper. **30.** The system by which the government regularly pays money to people who do not have a job, or are too old or ill to work.

On the road (pages 32 – 33)

Exercise 1:

1. (a) 17, (b) car, (c) motorcycle, (d) 18, (e) lorry, (f) 21, (g) lorry, (h) bus
2. (a) taxed, (b) tax disc, (c) insurance, (d) Third, (e) insurance, (f) comprehensive, (g) insurance, (h) penalties, (i) insurance, (j) fine, (k) disqualification, (l) 3, (m) MOT, (n) garage, (o) insurance, (p) invalid
3. (a) provisional, (b) motorcycle, (c) 125, (d) 21, (e) full, (f) 3, (g) provisional, (h) post office, (i) road tax
4. (a) learner, (b) L-plates, (c) public, (d) motorway
5. (a) full, (b) theory, (c) practical, (d) skills, (e) provisional, (f) full
6. (a) full, (b) European Union, (c) valid, (d) 12
7. (a) DVLA, (b) Driver, (c) Vehicle, (d) Licensing, (e) Agency

Additional information:

Note that once you have taxed your car (you can do this for 6 months or 12 months), the DVLA will automatically send you reminders to renew your tax when it is due. If your car is not being used and is "off the road" for a long period of time, you do not have to pay road tax, but you must tell the DVLA if this is the case: a form called a SORN (Statutory Off-Road Notification) is attached to your road tax renewal form for this purpose.
The DVLA will *not* remind you when your car's MOT is due: this is your responsibility.
If you renew your road tax at the post office, you will need to show a certificate of insurance and (if your vehicle is over 3 years old), a valid MOT certificate. If you do not, they will not renew your road tax.

Exercise 2:

1. (a) miles / miles per hour (mph), (b) 1 mile = approximately 1.609 kilometres **2.** False: all the passengers must wear seatbelts **3.** (a) Crash helmets, (b) Followers of the *Sikh* faith do not need to wear a helmet (if they are wearing their turban) **4.** (a) 30mph, (b) 60mph, (c) and (d) 70mph **5.** *Give way* means that you must give priority to other vehicles on the road (for example, at the junction of a road that you want to join, at a roundabout where other vehicles are coming from your right, etc) **6.** False. We drive on the *left*. **7.** (a) Yes, he is. You cannot use a hand-held mobile phone while you are driving your car (or even when your car is stopped but the engine is still running, in a traffic-jam for example). If the police catch you using one, you will probably get an *on-the-spot* (= instant) fine, and may get *penalty points* on your licence. (b) Yes, she is. If you use a mobile phone while driving, the phone must not be connected to the driver in any way. You must use a *wireless headpiece*). **8.** A *Breathalyser* ™ is a piece of equipment that the police use to see if a driver has been drinking alcohol. They will use it to perform a *breath test* if they think a driver has had more than the permitted amount of alcohol. Penalties are severe if the test is *positive* and the driver is *over the limit* (= they have exceeded the permitted amount): an automatic *disqualification* from driving of at least one year is usually the minimum penalty. A driver can be arrested if he / she has a positive breath test or if he / she refuses to do a breath test. **9.** 999 or 112. These are the numbers for the *emergency services* (police, ambulance, fire, coastguard, etc). **10.** Yes: a *hit-and-run* is an accident in which you hit a pedestrian or cyclist and fail to stop at the scene of the accident. It is an offence if you fail to stop when you are involved in any accident. **11.** Their name, address, vehicle registration number and insurance details (i.e., the name of their motor insurance company). It is also a good idea to make a note of their vehicle make and colour. **12.** Among other things, you should not admit that the accident was your fault. Your insurance company will decide this, based on the information you must give them. **13.** *Tailgating* is when you drive too close to the vehicle in front of you. UK drivers say being *tailgated* is the thing that makes them most angry. **14.** After checking that it is safe to pull out, you should always thank the driver with a quick wave of your hand. Most drivers in the UK are courteous, and expect the same from other road users: they can get quite angry if another road user fails to thank them for small acts of courtesy! **15.** (b). *The Highway Code* (= a book of road rules that every road user needs to know) states that if you flash your lights, you are claiming right of way. However, most drivers in the UK ignore this rule! **16.** In one situation only: to let other road users know that you are there. It is an offence to use it for any other reason. **17.** Yes: the pedestrian has *right of way*. **18.** (a) speeding, (b) joyriding (= the crime of stealing a car and driving it for pleasure), (c) disqualify, (d) overtake, (e) reverse, f) indicate, g) brake, h) roundabout (note that we go around a roundabout *clockwise*, and must give way to vehicles coming from the right), i) traffic lights, j) pedestrian crossing, k) junction, l) crossroads, m) speed camera, n) traffic calming (= bollards, bumps, etc, that prevent people from driving too fast in built-up areas).

UK places, people and institutions (pages 34 – 35)

Exercise 1:
Towns and cities in England: Birmingham, Bristol, Liverpool, York.
Towns and cities in Wales: Aberystwyth, Cardiff, Newport, Swansea.
Towns and cities in Scotland: Aberdeen, Edinburgh, Glasgow, Inverness.
Towns and cities in Northern Ireland: Armagh, Belfast, Londonderry (often called *Derry*), Omagh.
Counties: Cornwall, Kent, Northumberland, Oxfordshire.
Rivers: Clyde, Severn, Thames, Tyne.
National Parks: Dartmoor, Lake District, The North York Moors, the Pembrokeshire Coast.
Lakes: (Lough) Neagh, (Loch) Ness, (Lake) Ullswater, (Lake) Windermere (which is also the name of the town by the lake).

Exercise 2:
Banks: Barclays, HSBC, Lloyds TSB, NatWest (= *National Westminster*).
Supermarkets: Asda, Morrison's, Sainsbury, Tesco.
Department stores: BHS (*British Home Stores*), Debenhams, John Lewis, Marks and Spencer (often shortened to *Marks* or *M and S* in spoken English).
Places to eat: Ask, Beefeater, Harvester, Little Chef.
Airlines: British Airways, BMIbaby, Easyjet, Virgin Atlantic.
London airports: Gatwick, Heathrow, Luton, Stansted.
British seaports: Dover, Harwich, Liverpool, Southampton.
Museums and galleries: Ashmolean (Oxford), Hunterian (Glasgow), Tate Modern (London), Victoria and Albert (London).

Exercise 3:
Newspapers: The Guardian, The Independent, The Telegraph, The Sun.
Sporting events: The Ashes (cricket. This is also held in Australia), The FA Cup Final (football), The Grand National (horse racing), The Royal Regatta (rowing).
Sporting venues: Newmarket (horse racing), Silverstone (motor racing), Wembley Stadium (football and athletics), Wimbledon (tennis). Note that *Newmarket* and *Wimbledon* are also often used to describe the events that are held there: "*When does Wimbledon begin this year?*"
National holidays: Boxing Day (26th December), Easter Monday (March or April), The first Monday in May, New Year's Day (1st January).
Traditional days: Guy Fawkes Night (5th November), Mothering Sunday (the 3rd Sunday before Easter), Remembrance Day (11th November, but normally observed on the Sunday before when this date falls during the week), Saint Valentine's Day (14th February).
Charity organisations: Oxfam, The Red Cross, The RSPCA, Save the Children.
Famous tourist sights: Canterbury Cathedral, Edinburgh Castle, Stonehenge, The Tower of London.
Common pub names: The Queen's Head, The Red Lion, The Rose and Crown, The White Hart.

Exercise 4:
Political parties: Conservative, Green, Labour, Liberal Democrat.
Government positions: The Chancellor of the Exchequer, The Foreign Secretary, The Home Secretary, The Leader of the Opposition.
Prime Ministers: David Lloyd George, Margaret Thatcher, Tony Blair, Winston Churchill.
Scientists and inventors: Charles Darwin, Isaac Newton, Michael Faraday, Tim Berners-Lee.
Main religions: Christianity, Islam, Hinduism, Judaism.
Famous writers: Charles Dickens, George Orwell, Graham Greene, J.K. Rowling.
Artists and composers: Benjamin Britten, Edward Elgar, John Constable, JMW Turner.
Television programmes: Coronation Street, Eastenders, Panorama, Newsnight.

Politics and government 1 (pages 36 – 38)

Across:
1. Home Office **5.** House of Lords (Note that the House of Lords can delay, but not prevent, legislation (*see 13*

Answer key

across) coming from the House of Commons.) **8.** first past the post **10.** eligible **12.** constituent **13.** legislation **20.** Member *of* Parliament **21.** electorate **22.** Question Time **24.** spin (a *spin doctor* is someone whose job is to give journalists information that makes a politician or organisation seem as good as possible) **26.** general election (Elections that are held to elect officials who provide public services in particular towns or areas are called *local elections*.) **29.** Home Secretary **30.** Cabinet (Cabinet decisions on important matters must be submitted to Parliament for approval.) **31.** Shadow Cabinet **33.** Speaker **34.** House *of* Commons **35.** Liberal Democrats

Down:

1. proportional **3.** Opposition (Its formal name is *Her Majesty's Loyal Opposition*.) **4.** Scottish* **6.** Foreign Office (Its full name is the *Foreign and Commonwealth Office*, often abbreviated in writing to *FCO*.) **7.** Leader *of the* Opposition **9.** democracy **11.** Downing Street (often used as a general expression that is used to refer to the Prime Minister and the government: "*We are currently waiting for a statement from Downing Street*") **14.** Chancellor *of the* Exchequer (responsible every year for setting the country's *budget*) **15.** constituency **16.** Prime Minister (often abbreviated to *the PM*) **17.** Foreign Secretary **18.** secret ballot **19.** by-election **23.** confidence **25.** constitution **27.** Whitehall (Although this is the name of a street, it also refers to the area where the government is based, including the *Houses of Parliament*. It is often used as a general word to describe all the government officials who work for the British government: "*We're still waiting for a decision from Whitehall*".) **28.** whip **32.** Assembly (Northern Ireland also has some independence, in the form of the *Northern Ireland Assembly*.)*

* There are more questions on the Scottish, Welsh, and Northern Ireland political systems in the *Politics and government 3* on page 41.

Politics and government 2 (pages 39 – 40)

1. (b) a lobby (this has a similar role to a pressure group, although a pressure group is generally seen as a voluntary group of ordinary citizens which is not affiliated to a particular organisation, trade, etc). **2.** (d) a judge cannot challenge the legality of a law passed by Parliament. **3.** (a) make his / her own judgement (and so "create" a law. This is a good example of how the common law system works in the UK). Also note that if a judge feels that a previous judgement in a similar case does not reflect modern society, he / she can make his / her own judgement (and so "change" an existing law). **4.** (c) the Lord Chancellor (who selects from nominations provided by existing judges). **5.** All of these. **6.** (d) the Metropolitan Police. **7.** (b), (c), and (d) Local councillors and magistrates (who form a 'police authority') and the Home Secretary. **8.** (a) the IPCC (The Independent Police Complaints Commission), although in the first instance you should complain directly to the police force responsible. Other people and groups you could contact for help and advice include your local Citizens' Advice office (CAB) and your local Member of Parliament (MP). **9.** (d) the Civil Service. People who work for the Civil Service are called civil servants. **10.** (a) and (d) professionalism and political neutrality. The civil service can *warn* government ministers if they think a policy is impractical, impossible, unnecessary or against the public interest, but ultimately they must put that policy into practice. **11.** (a) it must put the new government's policies into practice. **12.** All of these. Most areas have both county *and* district councils. Large towns and cities have just one council (borough, city or metropolitan). **13.** (a) local authorities. **14.** All of these (and many more. Telephone directories usually list the different departments that provide these services, and most councils have their own website providing further information). **15.** (b) a councillor. **16.** (b) they must be elected in local elections (and either have local connections with that area, work in or for that area, be on the local electoral register or rent / own property in that area). **17.** (a) local government services that must be provided because the central government says they must be provided. The services described in (b) are called "permissive services". In England and Wales, councils can only provide permissive services if central government legislation allows them to do so. In Scotland, they can provide them unless central government expressly forbids them. **18.** (a) and (c) the government (about 80%) and local people (about 20%). **19.** (c) men and women over 18 (lowered from 21 in 1969. Women achieved the right to vote in 1928). Your name must be on the *electoral register* to do this. **20.** (a) and (e) a general right to vote and the right to hold a British passport. However, Commonwealth citizens, and citizens of the Republic of Ireland can vote in all public elections if they are resident in the UK, and EU citizens who are resident in the UK can vote in local elections (but not in national parliamentary elections). **21.** (b) £500 for MPs and members of the Scottish Parliament and Welsh and Northern Ireland Assemblies, and £5000 for Members of the European Parliament. **22.** (b) at least 5%. **23.** All of these, although some MPs do not hold regular morning surgeries. Contact details for MPs, MEPs, MSPs and Assembly members can be found in the telephone directory. **24.** (a) it has fallen, especially among younger people, who complain that they have become 'alienated' by and from mainstream politics.

Politics and government 3 (page 41)

Here is the complete text, with the correct spellings in **bold**.

The process of taking power from a central **authority** or **government** and giving it to smaller, more local regions is called **devolution**. This began in the UK in 1997, with the result that since 1999 there has been an Assembly in **Wales** and a Parliament in **Scotland**.

The Welsh Assembly* and the Scottish Parliament have control over many local issues, but can only **debate** the policy and laws governing general **taxation**, social

Answer key

security, **defence** and foreign **affairs** (which are decided by central government in London).

The Scottish Parliament is based in **Edinburgh** (Scotland's **principal** city), and is funded by a **grant** from the UK government. Scotland has had some limited **autonomy** from London for quite a long time, but the decision to begin creating a **separate** Parliament did not happen until a national **referendum** in 1997. Unlike the Welsh Assembly (see the paragraph below), the Scottish Parliament can make its own laws (with exceptions such as those listed in the paragraph above), and even has some powers over national income tax **rates**. Also, unlike the Welsh Assembly and the UK Parliament, members (known as MSPs) are elected by a type of **proportional representation**.

The Welsh Assembly is based in **Cardiff** (the Welsh **capital**). Assembly members are chosen in **elections** which are held every four years. It makes its own decisions on many local issues and **policies** such as **education**, health services and the **environment**. Although the Assembly cannot *make* laws for Wales, it is able to **propose** laws to central UK Parliament in **Westminster** who can then discuss them and possibly create **legislation** based on those **proposals**.

The Northern Ireland Assembly, based at Stormont in **Belfast**, was formed after the two main **organisations** responsible for terrorist activity in the region (the *IRA* – the Irish **Republican** Army – and the *UDA* – the Ulster Defence **Association**) agreed to cease armed hostilities. In the *Good Friday Agreement* of 1998, the main political wings of these groups agreed to work together with other political parties in a power-**sharing** agreement which resulted in the formation of the Assembly. Its powers are similar to the Welsh Assembly. However, it can be (and occasionally has been) **suspended** by the central UK government if the political leaders fail to work together, or if they act against the interests of the **citizens** of Northern Ireland.

For most people in the UK, contact and dealings with the government are through organisations known as non-**departmental** public bodies. These include: spending agencies such as regional **health** authorities and higher education **funding councils**; trading bodies to raise **revenue**, such as *the National **Savings** and Investments* and the *Forestry **Commission***; quasi-**judicial** and prosecuting bodies, such as the ***Monopolies** and Mergers Commission*, the *Crown Prosecution Service* and the *IPCC* (see *Politics and Government 2* on page 39); Statutory **Advisory** Bodies to Ministers, such as the *Health and Safety Commission*, the *Equal **Opportunities** Commission* and the *Commission for **Racial** Equality*; development agencies, such as the *Highlands and **Islands** Development **Board*** in Scotland, and the *Welsh Development Agency*.

* Full name: *The National Assembly for Wales*.

In the pub (page 42)

1. Public house. **2.** They must have a licence which allows them to sell alcohol for drinking *on the premises* (= in the pub). **3.** He / She is the person who owns / manages the pub (and often holds the licence in number 2). **4.** It is an independent pub: it is not owned by a brewery (= a company that makes beer). **5.** 18 (or 16 if you are eating a meal in a part of a pub that is set aside for eating meals. However, they can only drink *beer*, *wine* or *cider*). Some pubs, especially in large towns and cities, will only serve alcohol to people who are 21 or over. **6.** Usually yes, if they are accompanied by someone who is at least 18 years old. However, many pubs will refuse to admit children in the evenings. Some pubs have family rooms where children are allowed with their parents. **7.** When this book was being written, you could smoke in pubs in England, Wales and Northern Ireland, but not in Scotland. From spring 2007 in Northern Ireland, and from summer 2007 in England, smoking will be banned in all pubs. **8.** You go directly to the bar. **9.** Bitter, lager and stout are varieties of beer. Cider is an alcoholic drink made from apples. Spirits are strong alcoholic drinks such as whisky, vodka and brandy. **10.** Pints and half pints (1 pint = 0.57 litres). **11.** A single = 25ml, a double = 50ml. **12.** Yes. They are called *soft drinks*. Many pubs also serve non-alcoholic beer **13.** You are buying a drink for yourself and for the friends you are with. You would be considered very rude if you were with other people and only bought a drink for yourself. **14.** He is suggesting that everyone in the group gives one person in the group a certain amount of money, and that money is used to buy *rounds*. **15.** You pay for drinks (and usually for food) as you buy them (but see number 16). **16.** You want to pay for everything when you leave the pub, instead of paying for everything separately. Many pubs will let you start a tab if you leave a credit or debit card behind the bar. **17.** No, although it would be considered rude to spend all evening with just one drink, especially if the pub is busy. **18.** No, but it is normal to offer to buy a drink for the bar person. He / she will usually just take the money for that drink instead, or use it to buy him / herself a drink later. **19.** No, we stand at the bar with everyone else and wait to be served. **20.** You should look hopeful and try to '*catch the bar person's eye*'. Some people also hold their money in front of them so that the bar person can see they are waiting to be served. Never whistle, click your fingers, shout or wave your hand in the air! **21.** Apologise, and offer to buy them another drink. **22.** Normally yes, but you should always ask first. **23.** Normally yes, but it depends on the kind of pub and where it is. Generally, people in pubs in villages and small towns are more receptive to starting a conversation than those in big towns or cities. **24.** He wants to know where the toilets are. A female customer would ask for the '*ladies*'. **25.** Pub grub is food (usually traditional pub food such as *shepherd's pie*, *ploughman's lunch* etc: see the section in this book on *Food*). Bar snacks are crisps, peanuts and other light '*nibbles*', but might also include sandwiches. **26.** Pubs that serve good quality food that you would normally expect to find in an expensive restaurant. **27.** The pub will stop serving alcohol in ten minutes. **28.** The pub has stopped serving alcohol and you have

Answer key

twenty minutes to finish your drinks. **29.** 11pm, but many pubs can apply, or have applied, for an *extended licence*, which means that they can serve alcohol later than 11 o'clock. Some pubs will apply for a *temporary* extended licence for special occasions, such as a party. **30.** Yes: pubs are usually licensed to sell alcohol for consumption *off the premises*. **31.** Traditional pub games. **32.** You must leave the pub and not return, because you have said or done something bad. In some cases, if you are barred from one pub, you might automatically find yourself barred from other pubs in the area. **33.** Yes. Many pubs specify in writing that *service is at the discretion of the management*, which means they do not have to give a reason. However, most decent bar workers will normally tell you why they are refusing to serve you. In most cases this will be because you are (or look) too young and do not have ID (= identification) to prove otherwise, are inappropriately dressed, have already had too much to drink or are *barred* (see number 32). **34.** *Binge drinking* is where someone (usually a young man or woman) drinks a lot of alcohol very quickly and becomes very drunk. Binge drinking often results in fights, accidents and other problems.

Relationships 1: Marriage and related issues (page 43)

1. False. It is called a *marriage*. An *engagement* is when a man and woman announce their intention to get married. **2.** No. **3.** (a) 16, (b) 18*. **4.** Yes. **5.** Yes, but nobody can be forced to marry *against their will*. **6.** spouse. **7.** False. Generally a partner is someone you live with (and with whom you have a sexual relationship), although some people do refer to their spouse as their partner. **8.** 16 (the *age of consent* is the age at which couples are allowed to have a sexual relationship). **9.** No. Same-sex relationships are legal. **10.** No. Same-sex partners sometimes go through a marriage ceremony in countries where this is allowed, but the marriage will not be recognised in the UK. However, a recently-introduced *Civil Partnerships bill* gives same-sex couples many of the same rights and responsibilities as married couples. Same-sex couples have to register their commitment in a *civil ceremony*. **11.** No. A marriage must be *monogamous* (a man can only have one wife, and vice versa). **12.** Certificates from the *Registrar of Marriages* in the districts in which they live. **13.** No, although it is customary. **14.** Yes. **15.** (a) religious worship, (b) registry office, (c) local authority. **16.** No. **17.** A *separation* (from the verb *to separate*) is the state of two married people no longer living with each other. A *divorce* is the legal termination of a marriage (divorce can also be a verb: *to divorce*). **18.** Yes, and has been able to do so since 1857. **19.** They cannot divorce within one year of getting married. **20.** Yes, unless there are sound reasons why she cannot have children (for example, for health reasons). A woman can divorce her husband for the same reason. **21.** Yes. A man or woman who physically attacks his / her partner can be accused of *assault* or *grievous bodily harm*. **22.** Yes.

18 is called the *age of majority* in the UK. When a person becomes 18, he / she can marry without his / her parents' permission, vote in an election, buy and drink alcohol in a public place, etc.

Relationships 2: Children and related issues (page 44)

1. (a) The mother (unless the father marries the mother after the birth, gets the mother's agreement to have *joint responsibility*, obtains parental responsibility by applying to a court, or jointly registers the birth with the mother). Married couples have joint parental responsibility. **2.** (b) Until the child is 18. **3.** (c) Both of them (even if the couple separate). **4.** It depends on many issues, but in most cases the mother gets custody. However, unless there are adverse circumstances, the father should have *access* to his children on a regular basis (in other words, he sees his children, he takes them out, they stay at his home, etc). **5.** Yes, but the use of *force* must be reasonable (in other words, they should not smack them too hard or they could be prosecuted for assault. Alternatively, the child could be taken into the care of the local authority). **6.** Yes, in extreme circumstances (for example, if the child is in physical danger from one or both parents, if the child is not being fed and clothed properly, etc). **7.** (a) child support or (b) child maintenance. **8.** Yes. **9.** Child Support Agency. **10.** (c) 17. **11.** No, as long as the doctor or nurse believes the child understands what is involved. **12.** Yes, although they will encourage that person to discuss the issues involved with a parent. **13.** Yes. Children under the age of 16 should be left in the care of a responsible person who is aged 16 or over. **14.** No. Children under 16 are not allowed to work before 7 in the morning and after 7 in the evening. **15.** No. Three laws are being broken: (1) Children below the age of 14 cannot do paid work. (2) Children below the age of 17 cannot work in a kitchen. (3) Children under the age of 16 cannot work for more than one hour before school. **16.** No. Young people below the age of 16 cannot sell cigarettes or alcohol. Those aged 16 or 17 *can* sell alcohol in a shop, provided each individual sale has the approval of someone aged 18 or over. **17.** No, people are allowed to smoke from the age of 16. **18.** No, it is legal to drive a car from the age of 17 (with a qualified driver over 21 until you pass your test).

Shopping and consumerism (pages 45 – 46)

Exercise 1:

1. Waterstones **2.** The Link **3.** Boots **4.** Marks and Spencer (often simply called *Marks* by shoppers) **5.** Holland and Barrett **6.** Hallmark **7.** Cargo **8.** Next **9.** W.H. Smith (often simply called *Smith's* by shoppers) **10.** Clarks **11.** Prêt a Manger **12.** Starbucks **13.** Dixons **14.** Robert Dyas **15.** Specsavers **16.** HMV **17.** Thomas Cook **18.** Tesco **19.** Argos **20.** Barclays

Exercise 2:

1. responsibilities and liabilities **2.** satisfactory quality / 'as described' / 'fit for purpose' **3.** guarantee or warranty **4.** within a reasonable time / wear and tear **5.** proof of purchase / receipt **6.** defective / give a refund / credit voucher **7.** cooling-off period **8.** accurate description / delivery arrangements **9.** credit card fraud / opt out of / unsolicited mail / unsolicited telemarketing / written confirmation **10.** specified period **11.** claim for compensation **12.** reasonable care and skill / poor workmanship / reasonable charge

Signs and notices (pages 47 – 48)

1. On a bus or at a bus stop. **2.** In a bank. **3.** In a supermarket (at the checkout. Or there might be a sign that says '*6 / 8 / 10 (etc) items or less / fewer*'. **4.** Outside a hotel (usually a smaller, private hotel) or guest house. **5.** By the side of the road (usually on a busy road, where your stopped vehicle might cause a delay). **6.** On or outside a commercial or residential building: the building is vacant, and you can rent it. **7.** In a car park: you must buy a ticket from a machine and put it inside your car windscreen). **8.** On the packet or bottle of a pharmaceutical product: you should not eat or drink this product. **9.** By the side of the road (usually on a gate or garage door: the owner does not want you to park there). **10.** At a bus stop. **11.** Outside a piece of private land: if you go onto this land, the owner might take legal action against you. **12.** In a library or hospital (or any other place where you should not make a noise). **13.** On a machine or toilet door: you cannot use it because it is broken. **14.** In a shop (cards = credit cards). **15.** On a shop window (it might also say *Final sale* or *Clearance sale*). **16.** On an envelope or a parcel (which contains something that might break easily). **17.** In a supermarket (at the *fresh food counter*, where they might be a large group of people waiting to be served. You might also see this sign in other situations where a large group of people are waiting for service). **18.** and **19.** At the entrance to a toilet (*Gents = gentlemen*). **20.** On the packet or bottle of a pharmaceutical product: you are being warned not to take too much of it. **21.** On a fire alarm. **22.** In a public area such as a shopping centre or park. **23.** On your car windscreen: you have just received a parking ticket). **24.** On a wall or other flat surface: you must not put advertising posters and signs on this wall. **25.** Outside a hotel or guest house. A *B&B* is a *bed and breakfast*, a type of small, privately-owned hotel / guest house which is very common all over the UK. **26.** On the emergency alarm on a train (for example, on the underground. You will be fined if you pull the alarm without a good reason). **27.** On a wall or other empty surface (that has just been painted: you are being warned not to touch it). **28.** In a public area such as a shopping centre or park. **29.** On an envelope or parcel (that contains something that might break easily). **30.** By the side of the road: you are being told to drive more slowly. **31.** On the London Underground (specifically on the escalator, so that people can walk on the left side). **32.** By the side of the road: other traffic has priority over you. **33.** At a bus stop (or other places where you are expected to queue and it is not obvious *where* you should do this). **34.** In a hotel. **35.** In a pub. **36.** At the zoo. **37.** In the entrance to a museum, theatre or cinema: *concessions* are reduced prices. **38.** In a shop: you are being warned not to steal anything. **39.** Outside a hotel or guest house (which has a bar that you can use even if you are not staying in the hotel). **40.** Outside a pub (which has 'entertainment' for its customers). **41.** By the side of the road: you cannot drive your car here. **42.** Outside a pub. **43.** At a bus stop / on a bus. **44.** In a car park / by the side of the road (where parking is limited to a fixed period of time: when you leave, you cannot return there for the time specified). **45.** In a pub (or anywhere else where you need to be a particular age to do something, in this case drink alcohol). **46.** Outside a pub: they can refuse to let you in. **47.** In a café. **48.** On the back of a lorry or commercial vehicle. This is usually followed by a telephone number you can call if you want to complain about the driver.

Spoken responses (pages 49 – 50)

1. well (we can say *I'm fine*, but not *I'm very fine*) **2.** weather (the speaker is not feeling very well) **3.** truth **4.** looking **5.** sorry **6.** Bless (the usual response when somebody *sneezes*) **7.** see **8.** worry **9.** leg (= *you're joking*) **10.** to (we can also say *you too*) **11.** home **12.** lips **13.** congratulations **14.** chin **15.** sleep **16.** rather (= a polite way of saying *no*) **17.** chance (= a very informal / impolite way of saying *no*) **18.** love **19.** eyeballs **20.** luck / fingers **21.** returns (we can also say *Happy birthday*) **22.** wood (= an expression we use when we hope that something will or won't happen) **23.** tongue **24.** cheese (we say *say cheese* when we are taking a photograph and we want someone to smile) **25.** port **26.** guest **27.** help **28.** bad or tough (we can also say *tough luck*) **29.** bird **30.** dreams **31.** on **32.** message **33.** fun **34.** beggars **35.** hair **36.** life (sometimes used as an imperative when we think that someone is very boring: "*Get a life!*") **37.** Dutch **38.** care (we can also say *look after yourself*. If we want someone to write / phone / text / email us, we might also say *keep in touch*) **39.** hands **40.** ears

The UK A – Z (pages 51 – 53)

Exercise 1:
1. b **2.** a **3.** a **4.** b **5.** a **6.** b **7.** a **8.** a **9.** a **10.** a **11.** a **12.** b **13.** b **14.** b **15.** a

Exercise 2:
1. a **2.** b **3.** b **4.** a **5.** b **6.** b **7.** a **8.** b **9.** b **10.** b **11.** b **12.** b **13.** a **14.** a **15.** b

Exercise 3:
1. b **2.** b **3.** a **4.** a **5.** a **6.** a **7.** b **8.** b **9.** a **10.** a **11.** b **12.** a **13.** b **14.** b **15.** a

Utilities and services (page 54)

1. According to the water companies, it is perfectly safe to drink. However, because it can be quite heavily *chlorinated*, many people prefer to drink bottled or filtered water. **2.** All of these. The water companies usually send you one bill, and you can either pay it all at

Answer key

once, or pay half when you receive the bill and the other half six months later (if you choose this option, the company will send you a reminder for the second half). Alternatively, you can *spread the cost* over 10 months, usually paying by *direct debit*. **3.** It depends. In some areas, you pay according to the size of your property, and in other areas you have a water meter which records the amount of water you use. Water companies try to encourage people to install a water meter in their home. **4.** It depends. Sometimes it is, sometimes it is not. **5.** 240 volts. Three-pin *plugs* with rectangular pins, connect electrical items to the mains. **6.** Most homes are supplied with gas. **7.** Different companies, all offering different price plans. It is quite common for a gas company to also supply electricity, and vice versa. It is possible to move between suppliers if you are not happy with the service you are currently receiving. **8.** Gas. *Transco* are also the people you should call if you smell gas in your home or in the street. Their telephone number in such a situation is 0800 111 999. For general enquiries (for example, if you want to know the name of the gas suppliers in your region), you can call 0870 608 1524. For information on electricity suppliers, you can call *Energywatch* on 0845 906 0708. **9.** British Telecom, although there are many other providers for both land-line and mobile telephone services. For many Internet services (especially broadband), you will need a British Telecom land-line in your home. **10.** Either of these numbers will connect you to the *emergency services*. **11.** Once a week, usually on the same day (although this often changes for the week immediately following a national holiday). This service is provided by the local council. **12.** Possible. In fact, people are being actively encouraged to recycle more. Many councils provide residents with special boxes for this, and these are collected during the week, usually on the same day as regular household rubbish. Most towns and villages also have *recycling banks* (usually in a car park) where you can take items to leave for recycling. **13.** You cannot do this. However, you can call your council to arrange for these to be collected. They sometimes make a charge for this. **14.** Council tax. The amount you pay usually depends on the size and value of the property. This amount is normally reduced by 25% if just one person (or one person and children under 18) lives in the property. Reductions are also made for people on low incomes or for people who are out of work and claiming benefits. **15.** All of these are possible. If you pay in instalments (from April to January), most councils will let you pay by direct debit. **16.** Household insurance that insures the building against fire, theft and accidental damage. **17.** Both of these are possible. However, evictions are only used as an extreme measure. Most offenders will be 'bound over to keep the peace', which means that they must behave properly and decently or face further legal action. **18.** Try to talk to your neighbour. You could also talk to other neighbours to see if they are being affected, and you can also ask for advice from your local authority. Do not call the police unless you feel that the situation is getting quickly out of hand or if your neighbour becomes abusive or violent.

Where are they? (pages 55 – 57)

Exercise 1:

1. (a) meter, (b) luggage, (c) change. They are in a taxi.

Additional notes:

Speaker 1 (the driver) calls speaker 2 (the passenger) '*mate*'. This is a very informal (usually friendly) way men have of addressing other men. If the driver wanted to be more polite, he would say '*sir*'. Women are often informally addressed as '*love*' or '*dear*', or more formally as '*madam*'. Be careful how and when you use words like '*mate*', '*love*' or '*dear*', as many people consider them to be too informal.

When Speaker 2 says 'Keep the change', he is giving the taxi driver a *tip*. A tip of 10 – 15% is acceptable and welcomed by taxi drivers, waiters, hotel staff, hairdressers, etc.

2. (a) return, (b) peak, (c) fare, (d) platform. They are at a railway station.

Additional notes:

A *return* ticket will take you to your destination and back. If you just want to go to your destination, ask for a *single* or *one way* ticket.

On trains, the *peak period* is usually in the morning during the working week (Monday – Friday) when people are going to work.

3. (a) room service, (b) checked in, (c) housekeeping, (d) reception, (e) mini bar. They are in a hotel (talking on the telephone).

4. (a) performance, (b) matinee, (c) circle, (d) stage. They are in a theatre.

Additional notes:

A *matinee* is a cinema or theatre performance in the afternoon. The *circle* is a seating area that is upstairs in a theatre, and the *stalls* are downstairs, closer to the stage. The *stage* is where the actors and actresses perform.

5. (a) packing, (b) cashback, (c) PIN. They are at a supermarket checkout.

Additional notes:

Maestro is the trademark name of a *debit card*, which you can use to buy things in a shop or take money out of a cash machine. Some larger supermarkets offer you *cashback* when you use a debit card, which means that they give you cash and add the amount to your shopping bill. A *PIN* is a *personal identification number*, a four-digit security number that you need to know when using a debit card: in shops, you enter these numbers into an electronic handset.

6. (a) round, (b) pints, (c) snacks, (d) bar, (e) yourself, (f) half. They are in a pub.

Additional notes:

When Speaker 2 says '*It's my round*', she is offering to buy drinks for herself and her friend. It is traditional, and usually expected, in pubs for friends to take it in turns to buy 'rounds' of drinks for each other.

In pubs, beer and cider (an alcoholic apple-based drink) is served in *pints* or *half pints*. A British pint is equivalent to 0.57 litres.

Snacks are light meals, such as sandwiches or burgers.

When Speaker 2 says to Speaker 3 (the person working behind the bar) '*And one for yourself?*', she is offering to buy him a drink. We do not give tips to people working behind the bar in a pub, but it is traditional to offer to buy

him / her a drink. He / she will probably not drink this immediately, but will do so later. He / she will add the cost of this drink to your total bill.
Also note that in a pub, you order your drinks from the bar (you do *not* sit down and wait to be served), and you pay for them when you get them, although some pubs might let you have a *tab*, and you pay for all the drinks (and any food) you have had when you leave.
If a pub is very busy, people are usually happy to share a table with others, as long as they are asked first. This would not normally be considered acceptable in a restaurant.

Exercise 2:
1. (a) prescription, (b) registered, (c) surgery,(d) GP. They are in a doctor's surgery, clinic or health centre.
Additional notes:
A *repeat prescription* is medicine that you use on a regular basis that you need a doctor's note for. Note that many medicines that you can normally buy directly from a chemist or pharmacist in your country may require a doctor's prescription in the UK.
A *GP* is a *general practitioner*, a doctor who deals with general health problems.
2. (a) pharmacist, (b) hay fever, (c) remedies, (d) allergy, (e) branded. They are in a chemist or pharmacy.
Additional notes:
Over-the-counter remedies are medicines that you do not need a doctor's prescription for, but may still need to be sold by a qualified *pharmacist*. Many of these are *branded* (they are made by major companies with well-known names), but most chemists sell their *own-brand* versions, which contain the same active ingredients, but which are usually much cheaper.
Hay fever is a common, harmless but unpleasant medical condition caused by flower and grass pollen that affects your nose and eyes. It is most common in the summer. Hay fever sufferers sneeze a lot and their eyes itch.
3. (a) reservation, (b) service, (c) dessert, (d) bill. They are in a restaurant.
Additional notes:
Meals in restaurants usually consist of three or more courses: the *starter*; the *main course*; the *dessert*. The starter and the main course are ordered together at the beginning of the meal, the dessert is ordered after you have had the main course.
4. (a) deposit, (b) balance, (c) account, (d) statement, (e) transactions, (f) withdrawal. They are in a bank or building society.
Additional notes:
Most banks are open from Monday to Friday from 9 o'clock to 5 o'clock, but in some smaller towns they might open later and close earlier. Some banks in bigger towns and cities also open on a Saturday morning.
The bank where you hold your bank account is known as your *branch*: "*Is your account at this branch?*"
5. (a) change, (b) pass, (c) seat, (d) shout. They are on a bus.
Additional notes:
Many bus services only accept the exact amount of money for the *fare*, and cannot give you change. If you do not have the right change, the bus driver should give you a *credit note* so that you can get your money back from the bus company.
Speaker 2 (the bus driver) says '*Take a seat*', which is an informal way of saying '*Sit down*', and '*I'll give you a shout*' which is an informal way of saying '*I'll tell you when something is ready or when I need you*' (in this case, he will tell Speaker 1 – the passenger – when the bus arrives at his destination).
6. (a) pump, (b) unleaded, (c) receipt. They are at a petrol station.
Additional notes:
Most petrol stations in the UK are *self-service*: you put the petrol in the car yourself, remember your pump number, then pay at the cash desk.

Exercise 3:
1. (a) first class, (b) scales, (c) road tax, (d) insurance, (e) application. They are in a post office.
Additional notes:
Post offices provide a wide range of services. In addition to sending letters, parcels, etc, you can buy things such as insurance and foreign currency, you can pay bills (the post office sometimes charges you for this), you can withdraw money and you can pay money into your bank account (again, a small charge may be made for this).
British post has a *two-tier* system: *first class* and *second class*. First class post is quicker but more expensive than second class post. You can also send post by *recorded* or *special delivery*, which means that the person receiving it has to sign for it and you can get a record of this: this is usually recommended for important or valuable items that you want to post.
Post is delivered by an organisation callled *The Royal Mail*. The cost of sending an item of post depends on how you send it, and on both the weight <u>and</u> size of that item.
2. (a) clamped, (b) ticket, (c) Park and Ride, (d) time limit, (e) bay, f) attendant. They are in a car park.
Additional notes:
Speaker 1's car has been *clamped*: a device has been put on one of the wheels to stop him driving his car. He will need to pay a *fine* before the *clamp* is removed.
Many major towns and cities have *Park and Ride* facilities. These are large car parks outside the town where you leave your car and then take a bus to the town centre.
Parking *regulations* are strictly *enforced* in many places. If you park in the wrong place or fail to buy a ticket, you car could be clamped or *towed away* (= removed to a car *pound)*.
3. (a) bags, (b) scales, (c) pack, (d) interfered, (e) boarding pass, (f) delay, (g) departure, (h) gate, (i) flight. They are at an airport check-in.
Additional notes:
Airport procedures are very strict, and it is important to allow yourself lots of time to *check in*, go through the *security* and *passport checks* and get to your departure gate. It can be especially slow at larger airports such as London-Heathrow.
4. (a) concessions, (b) senior citizens, (c) guide, (d) gallery, (e) exhibits. They are in a museum.
Additional notes:
Concessions are reduced-price tickets for certain groups of people in places such as museums, theatres, etc. *Senior citizens* are people who are more than 60 years old.
5. (a) enrol, (b) course, (c) booked, (d) waiting list,

Answer key

(e) prospectus. They are at a college (of further education).
Additional notes:
Colleges of Further Education (CFEs) are found in most large towns and cities, and offer a large variety of study courses. Most of these are *subsidised* by *local education authorities*, which means that courses are cheaper and more affordable than private educational institutes. A *prospectus* lists the different courses that you can do at the college.

A year in the UK: Traditions, holidays and other occasions 1 (page 58)

1. New Year's **2.** resolutions **3.** Scotland **4.** Epiphany **5.** twelfth night **6.** decorations **7.** Burns Night **8.** Robert Burns **9.** whisky **10.** haggis **11.** tatties and neeps **12.** Shrove Tuesday **13.** Pancake **14.** Ash Wednesday **15.** Lent **16.** Easter **17.** St Valentine's **18.** leap **19.** St David's **20.** Wales **21.** Welsh **22.** daffodil **23.** St Patrick's **24.** Ireland **25.** Irish **26.** forward **27.** British **28.** Summer **29.** Time (BST) **30.** Mothering **31.** Mothers' **32.** mothers

A year in the UK: Traditions, holidays and other occasions 2 (page 59)

1. Fools' (also called *All Fools' Day*) **2.** midday **3.** Good **4.** buns **5.** breakfast **6.** Sunday **7.** secular (= non-religious) **8.** eggs **9.** lamb **10.** Monday **11.** Northern Ireland **12.** Scotland **13.** birthday **14.** George's **15.** England **16.** white with a red cross (the English flag, or the flag of St George: do not confuse this with the more familiar *Union flag*, which is the flag of the United Kingdom, and combines elements of the four countries' national flags) **17.** Monday **18.** Morris **19.** maypole **20.** Monday **21.** Spring **22.** longest **23.** Midsummer Day **24.** Father's Day **25.** Boyne (often simply called *Orange Day*) **26.** protestants **27.** Scotland **28.** Northern Ireland

A year in the UK: Traditions, holidays and other occasions 3 (page 60)

The words you need to put in the grid are:
1. Guy Fawkes Night (Guido Fawkes – shortened to *Guy* – was the man who was guarding the explosives in the cellar of Parliament when the King's men discovered the plot. We often burn his *effigy* on top of our fire on Guy Fawkes Night) **2.** St Andrew's Day **3.** Greetings **4.** holly **5.** New Year's Eve (often celebrated with parties that last until early in the morning) **6.** turkey **7.** Scotland **8.** Hogmanay **9.** Bonfire Night **10.** Boxing Day **11.** mistletoe (a plant that couples traditionally kiss under at Christmas) **12.** sporting **13.** Remembrance Day (usually observed on the Sunday closest to 11th November, when the Queen and senior politicians hold a service in London which is shown live on television) **14.** Halloween **15.** silence

The person in the shaded vertical strip is *Father Christmas* (also called *Santa Claus*), a friendly mythical character who has a long beard and dresses in red. He visits houses during the night of December 24th / 25th and leaves presents for children (who sometimes hang a stocking or sack at the end of their bed or by the fire so that he can fill them with presents).

Note that other traditions and customs are observed by other cultural and religious groups in the UK, but are not considered 'national' days or events. Examples include Chinese New Year, Divali, Yom Kippur, Passover, Hannukah, Ramadan, Eid ul-Fitr, Purim, Orthodox Easter, etc.